**OLD MOORE'S**

# HOROSCOPE AND ASTRAL DIARY

# SAGITTARIUS

# OLD MOORE'S

# HOROSCOPE AND ASTRAL DIARY

# SAGITTARIUS

## foulsham
LONDON • NEW YORK • TORONTO • SYDNEY

W. Foulsham & Co. Ltd
for Foulsham Publishing Ltd
The Old Barrel Store, Drayman's Lane, Marlow, Bucks SL7 2FF

Foulsham books can be found in all good bookshops and direct from
www.foulsham.com

ISBN: 978-0-572-04639-2

A CIP record for this book is available from the British Library

Printed in Denmark by Nørhaven, Viborg

# CONTENTS

# INTRODUCTION

Astrology has been a part of life for centuries now, and no matter how technological our lives become, it seems that it never diminishes in popularity. For thousands of years people have been gazing up at the star-clad heavens and seeing their own activities and proclivities reflected in the movement of those little points of light. Across centuries countless hours have been spent studying the way our natures, activities and decisions seem to be paralleled by their predictable movements. Old Moore, a time-served veteran in astrological research, continues to monitor the zodiac and has produced the Astral Diary for 2017, tailor-made to your own astrological makeup.

*Old Moore's Astral Diary* is unique in its ability to get the heart of your nature and to offer you the sort of advice that might come from a trusted friend. It enables you to see in a day-by-day sense exactly how the planets are working for you. The diary section advises how you can get the best from upcoming situations and allows you to plan ahead successfully. There's also room on each daily entry to record your own observations or appointments.

While other popular astrology books merely deal with your astrological 'Sun sign', the Astral Diaries go much further. Every person on the planet is unique and Old Moore allows you to access your individuality in a number of ways. The front section gives you the chance to work out the placement of the Moon at the time of your birth and to see how its position has set an important seal on your overall nature. Perhaps most important of all, you can use the Astral Diary to discover your Rising Sign. This is the zodiac sign that was appearing over the Eastern horizon at the time of your birth and is just as important to you as an individual as is your Sun sign.

It is the synthesis of many different astrological possibilities that makes you what you are and with the Astral Diaries you can learn so much. How do you react to love and romance? Through the unique Venus tables and the readings that follow them, you can learn where the planet Venus was at the time of your birth. It is even possible to register when little Mercury is 'retrograde', which means that it appears to be moving backwards in space when viewed from the Earth. Mercury rules communication, so be prepared to deal with a few setbacks in this area when you see the sign ☿. The Astral Diary will be an interest and a support throughout the whole year ahead.

*Old Moore extends his customary greeting to all people of the Earth and offers his age-old wishes for a happy and prosperous period ahead.*

# THE ESSENCE OF SAGITTARIUS

*Exploring the Personality of*
*Sagittarius the Archer*

(23RD NOVEMBER – 21ST DECEMBER)

## What's in a sign?

Sagittarius is ruled by the large, expansive planet Jupiter, which from an astrological perspective makes all the difference to this happy-go-lucky and very enterprising zodiac sign. This is the sign of the Archer and there is a very good reason for our ancient ancestors having chosen the half-man, half-horse figure with its drawn bow. Not only are Sagittarians fleet-footed like a horse, but the remarks they make, like the arrow, go right to the target.

You love contentious situations and rarely shy away from controversy. With tremendous faith in your own abilities you are not easily kept down, and would usually find it relatively simple to persuade others to follow your course. Though you are born of a Fire sign, you are not as bullying as Aries can be, or as proud as a Leo. Despite this you do have a Fire-sign temper and can be a formidable opponent once you have your dander up.

You rarely choose to take the long route to any destination in life, preferring to drive forward as soon as your mind is made up. Communication comes easy to you and you add to your stock of weapons good intuitive insight and a capacity for brinkmanship that appears to know no bounds. At your best you are earnest, aspiring and honourable, though on the other side of the coin Sagittarians can make the best con artists of all!

What you hate most is to be discouraged, or for others to thwart your intentions. There is a slight tendency for you to use others whilst you are engaging in many of the schemes that are an intrinsic part of your life, though you would never deliberately hurt or offend anyone.

Sagittarian people are natural lovers of fun. When what is required is a shot of enthusiasm, or an immediacy that can cut right through the middle of any red tape, it is the Archer who invariably ends up in charge. When others panic, you come into your own, and you have an ability to get things done in a quarter of the expected time. Whether they are completed perfectly, however, is a different matter altogether.

## Sagittarius resources

Sagittarians appear to be the natural conjurors of the zodiac. The stage magician seems to draw objects from thin air, and it often appears that the Archer is able to do something similar. This is an intriguing process to observe, but somewhat difficult to explain. Sagittarians seem to be able to get directly to the heart of any matter, and find it easy to circumnavigate potential difficulties. Thus they achieve objectives that look impossible to observers – hence the conjuring analogy.

Just as the biblical David managed to defeat Goliath with nothing more than a humble pebble and a sling, Sagittarius also goes seemingly naked into battle. The Archer relies on his or her natural wit, together with a fairly instinctive intelligence, a good deal of common sense and a silver tongue. The patient observer must inevitably come to the conclusion that what really matters isn't what the Sagittarian can do, but how much they manage to get others to undertake on their behalf. In other words, people follow your lead without question. This quality can be one of your best resources and only fails when you have doubt about yourself, which fortunately is very rarely.

If other signs could sell refrigerators to Eskimos, you could add a deep-freeze complete with ice tray! This is one of the reasons why so many Archers are engaged in both advertising and marketing. Not only do you know what people want, you also have an instinctive ability to make them want whatever it is you have on offer.

It is likely that you would see nothing remotely mysterious about your ability to peer through to the heart of any matter. In the main you would refer to this as 'gut reaction', despite the fact that it looks distinctly magical to those around you. Fortunately this is part of your mystique, and even if you should choose to take someone for a complete ride, it is doubtful that they would end up disliking you as a result. You don't set out to be considered a genius, and you manage to retain the common touch. This is extremely important, for those with whom you have contacts actively want to help you because you are a 'regular guy'.

## Beneath the surface

People tend to be very complicated. Untangling their motives in any given situation is rarely easy. Psychologists have many theories regarding the working of the human psyche and philosophers have struggled with such matters for thousands of years. Clearly none of these people were looking at the zodiac sign of Sagittarius. Ask the average Archer why they did this or that thing and the chances are that you will get a reply something very similar to 'Well, it seemed like a good idea at the time'.

While many people might claim to be uncomplicated, at heart you genuinely are. Complications are something you try to avoid, even though some of your deals in life might look like a roll of barbed wire to those around you. In the main you keep your objectives as simple as possible. This is one of the reasons why it isn't particularly difficult for you to circumnavigate some of the potential pitfalls – you simply won't recognise that they exist. Setting your eyes on the horizon you set off with a jaunty step, refusing to acknowledge problems and, when necessary, sorting them out on the way.

Your general intention is to succeed and this fact permeates just about every facet of your life. Satisfaction doesn't necessarily come for you from a job well done, because the word 'well' in this context often isn't especially important. And when you have one task out of the way, you immediately set your sights on something else. Trying to figure out exactly why you live your life in the way you do, your psychological imperatives and ultimate intentions, costs you too much time, so you probably don't indulge in such idle speculation at all.

You have a warm heart and always want the best for everyone. It almost never occurs to you that other people don't think about things in the way you might and you automatically assume that others will be only too pleased to follow your lead. In the main you are uncomplicated, don't indulge in too many frills and fancies and speak your mind. There really isn't much difference between what you do in life, and what you think about your actions. This is not to infer that you are shallow, merely that you don't see much point in complicating the obvious with too much internal musing.

One of the main reasons why people like you so much is because the 'what you see is what you get' adage is more true in your case than in any other.

## Making the best of yourself

Always on the go and invariably looking for a new challenge, it isn't hard to see how Sagittarius makes the best of itself. This is a dynamic, thrusting sign, with a thirst for adventure and a great ability to think on its feet. As a child of Sagittarius you need the cut and thrust of an exciting life in order to show your true mettle. It doesn't do for you to sit around inactive for any length of time and any sort of enforced lay-off is likely to drive you to distraction.

In a career situation your natural proclivities show through, so it's best for you to be in some position which necessitates decision making on a moment-by-moment basis. Production-line work or tasks that involve going over the same ground time and again are not really your forte, though you are certainly not afraid of hard work and can labour on regardless towards any objective – just as long as there is a degree of excitement on the way.

Socially speaking you probably have many friends, and that's the way you like things to be. You need to know that people rate you highly, and will usually be on hand to offer the sort of advice that is always interesting, but probably not totally reasoned. It's a fact that you think everyone has the same ability to think on their feet that typifies your nature, and you trust everyone instinctively – at least once.

In love you need the sort of relationship that allows a degree of personal freedom. You can't be fettered and so have to be your own person under all situations. You are kind and attentive, though sometimes get carried away with the next grand scheme and so you need an understanding partner. Archers should not tie themselves down too early in life and are at their best surrounded by those who love the dynamism and difficult-to-predict qualities exemplified by this zodiac sign.

Most important of all you need to be happy with your lot. Living through restricted or miserable times takes its toll. Fortunately these are few in your life, mainly because of the effort you put into life yourself.

## The impressions you give

You must be doing something right because it's a fact that Sagittarius represents one of the most instinctively liked zodiac signs. There are many reasons for this state of affairs. For starters you will always do others a good turn if it's possible. It's true that you are a bit of a rogue on occasions, but that only endears you to the sort of individuals with whom you choose to share your life. You are always the first with a joke, even under difficult circumstances, and you face problems with an open mind and a determination to get through them. On the way you acquire many friends, though in your case many 'acquaintances' might be nearer the mark. This is a situation of your own choosing and though you have so much to recommend you to others, it's a fact that you keep really close ties to the absolute minimum.

Some people might think you rather superficial and perhaps an intellectual lightweight. If so, this only comes about because they don't understand the way your mind works. All the same it is your own nature that leads a few individuals to these conclusions. You can skip from one subject to another, are an insatiable flirt in social situations and love to tell funny stories. 'Depth' isn't really your thing and that means that you could appear to lower the tone of conversations that are getting too heavy for your liking. You do need to be the centre of attention most of the time, which won't exactly endear you to others who have a similar disposition.

People know that you have a temper, like all Fire signs. They will also realise that your outbursts are rare, short-lived and of no real note. You don't bear a grudge and quickly learn that friends are more useful than enemies under any circumstance.

You come across as the capricious, bubbly, lively, likeable child of the zodiac and under such circumstances it would be very difficult for anyone to find fault with you for long. Often outrageous, always interesting and seldom down in the dumps – it's hard to see how you could fail to be loved.

## The way forward

It might be best to realise, right from the outset, that you are not indestructible. Deep inside you have all the same insecurities, vulnerabilities and paranoia that the rest of humanity possesses. As a Sagittarian it doesn't do to dwell on such matters, but at least the acknowledgement might stop you going over the edge sometimes. You come from a part of the zodiac that has to be active and which must show itself in the best possible light all the time, and that's a process that is very demanding.

In the main, however, you relish the cut and thrust of life and it is quite likely that you already have the necessary recipe for happiness and success. If you don't, then you are involved in a search that is likely to be both interesting and rewarding, because it isn't really the objective that matters to you but rather the fun you can have on the way.

Be as honest as you can with those around you, though without losing that slightly roguish charm that makes you so appealing. At the same time try to ensure that your own objectives bear others in mind. You can sometimes be a little fickle and, in rare circumstances, unscrupulous. At heart though, you have your own moral convictions and would rarely do anyone a bad turn. On the contrary, you do your best to help those around you, and invariably gain in popularity on the way.

Health-wise you are probably fairly robust but you can run your nervous system into the ground on occasions. There are times when a definite routine suits you physically, but this doesn't always agree with your mental make-up, which is essentially driving and demanding. The peaks and troughs of your life are an inevitable part of what makes you tick, and you would be a poorer person without them.

Explaining yourself is not generally difficult, and neither is the search for personal success, even if you keep looking beyond it to even greater achievements further down the road. Being loved is important, despite the fact that you would deny this on occasions. Perhaps you don't always know yourself as well as you might, though since you are not an inveterate deep thinker it is likely that this is not a problem to you.

If you are already an adult, it's likely the path you are presently following is the one for you. That doesn't mean to say that you will keep to it, or find it universally rewarding. You find new promise in each day, and that's the joy of Sagittarius.

# SAGITTARIUS ON THE CUSP

Old Moore is often asked how astrological profiles are altered for those people born at either the beginning or the end of a zodiac sign, or, more properly, on the cusps of a sign. In the case of Sagittarius this would be on the 23rd of November and for two or three days after, and similarly at the end of the sign, probably from the 19th to the 21st of December. In this year's Astral Diaries, once again, Old Moore sets out to explain the differences regarding cuspid signs.

## The Scorpio Cusp – November 23rd to 25th

You could turn out to be one of the most well-liked people around, especially if you draw heavily from the more positive qualities of the two zodiac signs that have the most profound part to play in your life. Taken alone the Sagittarian is often accused of being rather too flighty. Sagittarians are often guilty of flirting and sometimes fall foul of people who take a more serious view of life in general. The presence in your make-up of the much deeper and more contemplative sign of Scorpio brings a quiet and a sense of reserve that the Sagittarian nature sometimes lacks. Although you like to have a good time and would be more than willing to dance the night away, you are probably also happy enough when the time comes to go home. Family means much to you and you have a great sensitivity to the needs of those around you. What makes all the difference is that you not only understand others, but you have the potential to take practical steps to help them.

You are probably not quite the workaholic that the Archer alone tends to be and can gain rest and relaxation, which has to be good for you in the longer term. You don't lack the ability to be successful but your level of application is considered, less frenetic and altogether more ordered. It's true that some confusion comes into your life from time to time, but you have the resources to deal with such eventualities, and you do so with a smile on your face most of the time. People would warm to you almost instantly and you are likely to do whatever you can to support family members and friends.

Often sinking into a dream world if you feel threatened, some of the achievements that are second nature to the Sagittarian are left on the shelf for a while. There are times when this turns out to be a blessing, if only because your actions are more considered. Personality clashes with others are less likely with this combination and Sagittarius also modifies the slightly moody qualities that come with Scorpio alone. More methodical in every way than the usual Archer, in many situations you are a good combination of optimist and pessimist.

# The Capricorn Cusp – December 19th to 21st

The fact that comes across almost immediately with the Capricorn cusp of Sagittarius is how very practical you tend to be. Most of you would be ideal company on a desert island, for a number of reasons. Firstly you are quite self-contained, which Sagittarius taken alone certainly is not. You would soon get your head round the practical difficulties of finding food and shelter, and would be very happy to provide these necessities for your companions too. Unlike the typical Sagittarian you do not boast and probably do not come across as being quite so overbearing as the Archer seems to be. For all this you are friendly, chatty, love to meet many different and interesting types and do whatever you can to be of assistance to a world which is all the better for having you in it.

There is less of a tendency for you to worry at a superficial level than Sagittarius alone is inclined to do, mainly because long periods of practical application bring with them a contemplative tendency that Sagittarius sometimes lacks. In love you tend to be quite sincere, even if the slightly fickle tendencies of the Archer do show through now and again. Any jealousy that is levelled at you by your partner could be as a result of your natural attractiveness, which you probably don't seek. Fairly comfortable in almost any sort of company, you are at your best when faced with individuals who have something intelligent and interesting to say. As a salesperson you would be second to none, but it would be essential for you to believe absolutely in the product or service you were selling.

Almost any sort of work is possible in your case, though you wouldn't take too kindly to being restricted in any way, and need the chance to show what your practical nature is worth, as well as your keen perception and organisational abilities. What matters most for you at work is that you are well liked by others and that you manage to maintain a position of control through inspiring confidence. On a creative level, the combination of Sagittarius and Capricorn would make you a good sculptor, or possibly a natural landscape gardener.

# SAGITTARIUS AND ITS ASCENDANTS

The nature of every individual on the planet is composed of the rich variety of zodiac signs and planetary positions that were present at the time of their birth. Your Sun sign, which in your case is Sagittarius, is one of the many factors when it comes to assessing the unique person you are. Probably the most important consideration, other than your Sun sign, is to establish the zodiac sign that was rising over the eastern horizon at the time that you were born. This is your Ascending or Rising sign. Most popular astrology fails to take account of the Ascendant, and yet its importance remains with you from the very moment of your birth, through every day of your life. The Ascendant is evident in the way you approach the world, and so, when meeting a person for the first time, it is this astrological influence that you are most likely to notice first. Our Ascending sign essentially represents what we appear to be, while the Sun sign is what we feel inside ourselves.

The Ascendant also has the potential for modifying our overall nature. For example, if you were born at a time of day when Sagittarius was passing over the eastern horizon (this would be around the time of dawn) then you would be classed as a double Sagittarius. As such, you would typify this zodiac sign, both internally and in your dealings with others. However, if your Ascendant sign turned out to be an Earth sign, such as Taurus, there would be a profound alteration of nature, away from the expected qualities of Sagittarius.

One of the reasons why popular astrology often ignores the Ascendant is that it has always been rather difficult to establish. Old Moore has found a way to make this possible by devising an easy-to-use table, which you will find on page 125 of this book. Using this, you can establish your Ascendant sign at a glance. You will need to know your rough time of birth, then it is simply a case of following the instructions.

For those readers who have no idea of their time of birth it might be worth allowing a good friend, or perhaps your partner, to read through the section that follows this introduction. Someone who deals with you on a regular basis may easily discover your Ascending sign, even though you could have some difficulty establishing it for yourself. A good understanding of this component of your nature is essential if you want to be aware of that 'other person' who is responsible for the way you make contact with the world at large. Your Sun sign, Ascendant sign, and the other pointers in this book will, together, allow you a far better understanding of what makes you tick as an individual. Peeling back the different layers of your astrological make-up can be an enlightening experience, and the Ascendant may represent one of the most important layers of all.

## Sagittarius with Sagittarius Ascendant

You are very easy to spot, even in a crowd. There is hardly a more dynamic individual to be found anywhere in the length and breadth of the zodiac. You know what you want from life and have a pretty good idea about how you will get it. The fact that you are always so cocksure is a source of great wonder to those around you, but they can't see deep inside, where you are not half as certain as you appear to be. In the main you show yourself to be kind, attentive, caring and a loyal friend. To balance this, you are determined and won't be thwarted by anything.

You keep up a searing pace through life and sometimes find it difficult to understand those people who have slightly less energy. In your better moments you understand that you are unique and will wait for others to catch up. Quite often you need periods of rest in order to recharge batteries that run down through over-use, but it doesn't take you too long to get yourself back on top form. In matters of the heart you can be slightly capricious, but you are a confident lover who knows the right words and gestures. If you are ever accused of taking others for granted you might need to indulge in some self-analysis.

## Sagittarius with Capricorn Ascendant

The typical Sagittarian nature is modified for the better when Capricorn is part of the deal. It's true that you manage to push forward progressively under most circumstances, but you also possess staying power and can work long and hard to achieve your objectives, most of which are carefully planned in advance. Few people have the true measure of your nature, for it runs rather deeper than appears to be the case on the surface. Routines don't bother you as much as would be the case for Sagittarius when taken alone, and you don't care if any objective takes weeks, months or even years to achieve. You are very fond of those you take to, and prove to be a capable friend, even when things get tough.

In love relationships you are steadfast and reliable, and yet you never lose the ability to entertain. Yours is a dry sense of humour which shows itself to a multitude of different people and which doesn't evaporate, even on those occasions when life gets tough. It might take you a long time to find the love of your life, but when you do there is a greater possibility of retaining the relationship for a long period. You don't tend to inherit money, but you can easily make it for yourself, though you don't worry too much about the amount. On the whole you are self-sufficient and sensible.

## Sagittarius with Aquarius Ascendant

There is an original streak to your nature which is very attractive to the people with whom you share your life. Always different, ever on the go and anxious to try out the next experiment in life, you are interested in almost everything and yet deeply attached to almost nothing. Everyone you know thinks that you are a little 'odd', but you probably don't mind them believing this because you know it to be true. In fact it is possible that you positively relish your eccentricity, which sets you apart from the common herd and means that you are always going to be noticed.

Although it may seem strange with this combination of Air and Fire, you can be distinctly cool on occasions, have a deep and abiding love of your own company now and again, and won't easily be understood. Love comes fairly easily to you but there are times when you are accused of being self-possessed, self-indulgent and not willing enough to fall in line with the wishes of those around you. Despite this you walk on and on down your own path. At heart you are an extrovert and you love to party, often late into the night. Luxury appeals to you, though it tends to be of the transient sort. Travel could easily play a major and a very important part in your life.

## Sagittarius with Pisces Ascendant

A very attractive combination this, because the more dominant qualities of the Archer are somehow mellowed-out by the caring Water-sign qualities of the Fishes. You can be very outgoing, but there is always a deeper side to your nature that allows others to know that you are thinking about them. Few people could fall out with either your basic nature or your attitude to the world at large, even though there are depths to your personality that may not be easily understood. You are capable, have a good executive ability and can work hard to achieve your objectives, even if you get a little disillusioned on the way. Much of your life is given over to helping those around you and there is a great tendency for you to work for and on behalf of humanity as a whole. A sense of community is brought to most of what you do and you enjoy co-operation.

Although you have the natural Sagittarian ability to attract people to you, the Pisces half of your nature makes you just a little more reserved in personal matters than might otherwise be the case. More careful in your choices than either sign taken alone, you still have to make certain that your motivations when commencing a personal relationship are the right ones. You love to be happy, and to offer gifts of happiness to others.

## Sagittarius with Aries Ascendant

What a lovely combination this can be, for the devil-may-care aspects of Sagittarius lighten the load of a sometimes too serious Aries interior. Everything that glistens is not gold, though it's hard to convince you of the fact because, to mix metaphors, you can make a silk purse out of a sow's ear. Almost everyone loves you, and in return you offer a friendship that is warm and protective, but not as demanding as sometimes tends to be the case with the Aries type. Relationships may be many and varied and there is often more than one major attachment in the life of those holding this combination. You can bring a breath of spring to any relationship, though you need to ensure that the person concerned is capable of keeping up with the hectic pace of your life.

It may appear from time to time that you are rather too trusting for your own good, though deep inside you are very astute, and it seems that almost everything you undertake works out well in the end. This has nothing to do with native luck and is really down to the fact that you are much more calculating than might appear to be the case at first sight. As a parent you are protective, yet offer sufficient room for self-expression.

## Sagittarius with Taurus Ascendant

A dual nature is evident here, and if it doesn't serve to confuse you it will certainly be a cause of concern to many of the people with whom you share your life. You like to have a good time and are a natural party-goer. On such occasions you are accommodating, chatty and good to know. But contrast this with the quieter side of Taurus, which is directly opposed to your Sagittarian qualities. The opposition of forces is easy for you to deal with because you inhabit your own body and mind all the time, but it's far less easy for friends and relatives to understand. As a result, on those occasions when you decide that, socially speaking, enough is enough, you will need to explain the fact to the twelve people who are waiting outside your door with party hats and whoopee cushions.

Confidence to do almost anything is not far from the forefront of your mind and you readily embark on adventures that would have some types flapping about in horror. Here again, it is important to realise that we are not all built the same way and that gentle coaxing is sometimes necessary to bring others round to your point of view. If you really have a fault, it could be that you are so busy being your own, rather less than predictable self, that you fail to take the rest of the world into account.

## Sagittarius with Gemini Ascendant

'Tomorrow is another day!' This is your belief and you stick to it. There isn't a brighter and more optimistic soul to be found than you and almost everyone you come into contact with is touched by the fact. Dashing about from one place to another, you manage to get more things done in one day than most other people would achieve in a week. Of course this explains why you are so likely to wear yourself out and it means that frequent periods of absolute rest are necessary if you are to remain truly healthy and happy. Sagittarius makes you brave and sometimes a little headstrong, so you need to curb your natural enthusiasm while you stop to think about the consequences of your actions.

It's not really certain if you do 'think' in the accepted sense of the word, because the lightning qualities of both these signs mean that your reactions are second to none. However, you are not indestructible and you put far more pressure on yourself than would often be sensible. Routines are not your thing at all, and many of you manage to hold down two or more jobs at once. It might be an idea to stop and smell the flowers on the way, and you could certainly do with putting your feet up much more than you do. However, you probably won't still be reading this passage because you will have something far more important to do!

## Sagittarius with Cancer Ascendant

You have far more drive, enthusiasm and get-up-and-go than would seem to be the case for Cancer when taken alone, but all of this is tempered with a certain quiet compassion that probably makes you the best sort of Sagittarian too. It's true that you don't like to be on your own or to retire in your shell quite as much as the Crab usually does, though there are, even in your case, occasions when this is going to be necessary. Absolute concentration can sometimes be a problem to you, though this is hardly likely to be the case when you are dealing with matters relating to your home or family, both of which reign supreme in your thinking. Always loving and kind, you are a social animal and enjoy being out there in the real world, expressing the deeper opinions of Cancer much more readily than would often be the case with other combinations relating to the sign of the Crab.

Personality is not lacking and you tend to be very popular, not least because you are the fountain of good and practical advice. You want to get things done and retain a practical approach to most situations which is the envy of many other people. As a parent you are second to none, combining common sense, dignity and a sensible approach. To balance this you stay young enough to understand children.

## Sagittarius with Leo Ascendant

Above and beyond anything else you are naturally funny, and this is an aspect of your nature that will bring you intact through a whole series of problems that you manage to create for yourself. Chatty, witty, charming, kind and loving, you personify the best qualities of both these signs, whilst also retaining the Fire-sign ability to keep going, long after the rest of the party has gone home to bed. Being great fun to have around, you attract friends in the way that a magnet attracts iron filings. Many of these will be casual connections but there will always be a nucleus of deep, abiding attachments that may stay around you for most of your life.

You don't often suffer from fatigue, but on those occasions when you do there is ample reason to stay still for a while and to take stock of situations. Routines are not your thing and you like to fill your life with variety. It's important to do certain things right, however, and staying power is something that comes with age, assisted by the Fixed quality of Leo. Few would lock horns with you in an argument, which you always have to win. In a way you are a natural debator but you can sometimes carry things too far if you are up against a worthy opponent. You have the confidence to sail through situations that would defeat others.

## Sagittarius with Virgo Ascendant

This is a combination that might look rather odd at first sight because these two signs have so very little in common. However, the saying goes that opposites attract, and in terms of the personality you display to the world this is especially true in your case. Not everyone understands what makes you tick but you try to show the least complicated face to the world that you can manage to display. You can be deep and secretive on occasions, and yet at other times you can start talking as soon as you climb out of bed and never stop until you are back there again. Inspirational and spontaneous, you take the world by storm on those occasions when you are free from worries and firing on all cylinders. It is a fact that you support your friends, though there are rather more of them than would be the case for Virgo taken on its own, and you don't always choose them as wisely as you might.

There are times when you display a temper, and although Sagittarius is incapable of bearing a grudge, the same cannot be said for Virgo, which has a better memory than the elephant. For the best results in life you need to relax as much as possible and avoid overheating that powerful and busy brain. Virgo gives you the ability to concentrate on one thing at once, a skill you should encourage.

## Sagittarius with Libra Ascendant

A very happy combination this, with a great desire for life in all its forms and a need to push forward the bounds of the possible in a way that few other zodiac sign connections would do. You don't like the unpleasant or ugly in life and yet you are capable of dealing with both if you have to. Giving so much to humanity, you still manage to retain a degree of individuality that would surprise many, charm others, and please all.

On the reverse side of the same coin you might find that you are sometimes accused of being fickle, but this is only an expression of your need for change and variety, which is intrinsic to both these signs. True, you have more of a temper than would be the case for Libra when taken on its own, but such incidents would see you up and down in a flash and it is almost impossible for you to bear a grudge of any sort. Routines get on your nerves and you are far happier when you can please yourself and get ahead at your own pace, which is quite fast.

As a lover you can make a big impression and most of you will not go short of affection in the early days, before you choose to commit yourself. Once you do, there is always a chance of romantic problems, but these are less likely when you have chosen carefully in the first place.

## Sagittarius with Scorpio Ascendant

There are many gains with this combination, and most of you reading this will already be familiar with the majority of them. Sagittarius offers a bright and hopeful approach to life, but may not always have the staying power and the patience to get what it really needs. Scorpio, on the other hand, can be too deep for its own good, is very self-seeking on occasions and extremely giving to others. Both the signs have problems when taken on their own, and, it has to be said, double the difficulties when they come together. But this is not usually the case. Invariably the presence of Scorpio slows down the over-quick responses of the Archer, whilst the inclusion of Sagittarius prevents Scorpio from taking itself too seriously.

Life is so often a game of extremes, when all the great spiritual masters of humanity have indicated that a 'middle way' is the path to choose. You have just the right combination of skills and mental faculties to find that elusive path, and can bring great joy to yourself and others as a result. Most of the time you are happy, optimistic, helpful and a joy to know. You have mental agility, backed up by a stunning intuition, which itself would rarely let you down. Keep a sense of proportion and understand that your depth of intellect is necessary in order to curb the more flighty aspects of Scorpio.

# THE MOON AND THE PART IT PLAYS IN YOUR LIFE

In astrology the Moon is probably the single most important heavenly body after the Sun. Its unique position, as partner to the Earth on its journey around the solar system, means that the Moon appears to pass through the signs of the zodiac extremely quickly. The zodiac position of the Moon at the time of your birth plays a great part in personal character and is especially significant in the build-up of your emotional nature.

## Sun Moon Cycles

The first lunar cycle deals with the part the position of the Moon plays relative to your Sun sign. I have made the fluctuations of this pattern easy for you to understand by means of a simple cyclic graph. It appears on the first page of each 'Your Month At A Glance', under the title 'Highs and Lows'. The graph displays the lunar cycle and you will soon learn to understand how its movements have a bearing on your level of energy and your abilities.

## Your Own Moon Sign

Discovering the position of the Moon at the time of your birth has always been notoriously difficult because tracking the complex zodiac positions of the Moon is not easy. This process has been reduced to three simple stages with Old Moore's unique Lunar Tables. A breakdown of the Moon's zodiac positions can be found from page 28 onwards, so that once you know what your Moon Sign is, you can see what part this plays in the overall build-up of your personal character.

If you follow the instructions on the next page you will soon be able to work out exactly what zodiac sign the Moon occupied on the day that you were born and you can then go on to compare the reading for this position with those of your Sun sign and your Ascendant. It is partly the comparison between these three important positions that goes towards making you the unique individual you are.

# HOW TO DISCOVER YOUR MOON SIGN

**T**his is a three-stage process. You may need a pen and a piece of paper but if you follow the instructions below the process should only take a minute or so.

**STAGE 1** First of all you need to know the Moon Age at the time of your birth. If you look at Moon Table 1, on page 26, you will find all the years between 1919 and 2017 down the left side. Find the year of your birth and then trace across to the right to the month of your birth. Where the two intersect you will find a number. This is the date of the New Moon in the month that you were born. You now need to count forward the number of days between the New Moon and your own birthday. For example, if the New Moon in the month of your birth was shown as being the 6th and you were born on the 20th, your Moon Age Day would be 14. If the New Moon in the month of your birth came after your birthday, you need to count forward from the New Moon in the previous month. If you were born in a Leap Year, remember to count the 29th February. You can tell if your birth year was a Leap Year if the last two digits can be divided by four. Whatever the result, jot this number down so that you do not forget it.

**STAGE 2** Take a look at Moon Table 2 on page 27. Down the left hand column look for the date of your birth. Now trace across to the month of your birth. Where the two meet you will find a letter. Copy this letter down alongside your Moon Age Day.

**STAGE 3** Moon Table 3 on page 27 will supply you with the zodiac sign the Moon occupied on the day of your birth. Look for your Moon Age Day down the left hand column and then for the letter you found in Stage 2. Where the two converge you will find a zodiac sign and this is the sign occupied by the Moon on the day that you were born.

## Your Zodiac Moon Sign Explained

You will find a profile of all zodiac Moon Signs on pages 28 to 31, showing in yet another way how astrology helps to make you into the individual that you are. In each daily entry of the Astral Diary you can find the zodiac position of the Moon for every day of the year. This also allows you to discover your lunar birthdays. Since the Moon passes through all the signs of the zodiac in about a month, you can expect something like twelve lunar birthdays each year. At these times you are likely to be emotionally steady and able to make the sort of decisions that have real, lasting value.

# Moon Table 1

| YEAR | OCT | NOV | DEC | YEAR | OCT | NOV | DEC | YEAR | OCT | NOV | DEC |
|------|-----|-----|-----|------|-----|-----|-----|------|-----|-----|-----|
| 1919 | 23 | 22 | 21 | 1952 | 18 | 17 | 17 | 1985 | 14 | 12 | 12 |
| 1920 | 12 | 10 | 10 | 1953 | 8 | 6 | 6 | 1986 | 3 | 2 | 1/30 |
| 1921 | 1/30 | 29 | 29 | 1954 | 26 | 25 | 25 | 1987 | 22 | 21 | 20 |
| 1922 | 20 | 19 | 18 | 1955 | 15 | 14 | 14 | 1988 | 10 | 9 | 9 |
| 1923 | 10 | 8 | 8 | 1956 | 4 | 2 | 2 | 1989 | 29 | 28 | 28 |
| 1924 | 28 | 26 | 26 | 1957 | 23 | 21 | 21 | 1990 | 18 | 17 | 17 |
| 1925 | 17 | 16 | 15 | 1958 | 12 | 11 | 10 | 1991 | 8 | 6 | 6 |
| 1926 | 6 | 5 | 5 | 1959 | 2/31 | 30 | 29 | 1992 | 25 | 24 | 24 |
| 1927 | 25 | 24 | 24 | 1960 | 20 | 19 | 18 | 1993 | 15 | 14 | 14 |
| 1928 | 14 | 12 | 12 | 1961 | 9 | 8 | 7 | 1994 | 5 | 3 | 2 |
| 1929 | 2 | 1 | 1/30 | 1962 | 28 | 27 | 26 | 1995 | 24 | 22 | 22 |
| 1930 | 20 | 19 | 19 | 1963 | 17 | 15 | 15 | 1996 | 11 | 10 | 10 |
| 1931 | 11 | 9 | 9 | 1964 | 5 | 4 | 4 | 1997 | 31 | 30 | 29 |
| 1932 | 29 | 27 | 27 | 1965 | 24 | 22 | 22 | 1998 | 20 | 19 | 18 |
| 1933 | 19 | 17 | 17 | 1966 | 14 | 12 | 12 | 1999 | 8 | 8 | 7 |
| 1934 | 8 | 7 | 6 | 1967 | 3 | 2 | 1/30 | 2000 | 27 | 26 | 25 |
| 1935 | 27 | 26 | 25 | 1968 | 22 | 21 | 20 | 2001 | 17 | 16 | 15 |
| 1936 | 15 | 14 | 13 | 1969 | 10 | 9 | 9 | 2002 | 6 | 4 | 4 |
| 1937 | 4 | 3 | 2 | 1970 | 1/30 | 29 | 28 | 2003 | 25 | 24 | 23 |
| 1938 | 23 | 22 | 21 | 1971 | 19 | 18 | 17 | 2004 | 12 | 11 | 11 |
| 1939 | 12 | 11 | 10 | 1972 | 8 | 6 | 6 | 2005 | 2 | 1 | 1/31 |
| 1940 | 1/30 | 29 | 28 | 1973 | 26 | 25 | 25 | 2006 | 21 | 20 | 20 |
| 1941 | 20 | 19 | 18 | 1974 | 15 | 14 | 14 | 2007 | 11 | 9 | 9 |
| 1942 | 10 | 8 | 8 | 1975 | 5 | 3 | 3 | 2008 | 29 | 28 | 27 |
| 1943 | 29 | 27 | 27 | 1976 | 23 | 21 | 21 | 2009 | 18 | 17 | 16 |
| 1944 | 17 | 15 | 15 | 1977 | 12 | 11 | 10 | 2010 | 8 | 8 | 6 |
| 1945 | 6 | 4 | 4 | 1978 | 2/31 | 30 | 29 | 2011 | 27 | 25 | 25 |
| 1946 | 24 | 23 | 23 | 1979 | 20 | 19 | 18 | 2012 | 15 | 13 | 12 |
| 1947 | 14 | 12 | 12 | 1980 | 9 | 8 | 7 | 2013 | 4 | 2 | 2 |
| 1948 | 2 | 1 | 1/30 | 1981 | 27 | 26 | 26 | 2014 | 22 | 22 | 1 |
| 1949 | 21 | 20 | 19 | 1982 | 17 | 15 | 15 | 2015 | 12 | 11 | 20 |
| 1950 | 11 | 9 | 9 | 1983 | 6 | 4 | 4 | 2016 | 30 | 29 | 29 |
| 1951 | 1/30 | 29 | 28 | 1984 | 24 | 22 | 22 | 2017 | 20 | 18 | 18 |

## Table 2

| DAY | NOV | DEC |
|-----|-----|-----|
| 1 | e | i |
| 2 | e | i |
| 3 | e | m |
| 4 | f | m |
| 5 | f | n |
| 6 | f | n |
| 7 | f | n |
| 8 | f | n |
| 9 | f | n |
| 10 | f | n |
| 11 | f | n |
| 12 | f | n |
| 13 | g | n |
| 14 | g | n |
| 15 | g | n |
| 16 | g | n |
| 17 | g | n |
| 18 | g | n |
| 19 | g | n |
| 20 | g | n |
| 21 | g | n |
| 22 | g | n |
| 23 | i | q |
| 24 | i | q |
| 25 | i | q |
| 26 | i | q |
| 27 | i | q |
| 28 | i | q |
| 29 | i | q |
| 30 | i | q |
| 31 | – | q |

## Table 3

| M/D | e | f | g | i | m | n | q |
|-----|-----|-----|-----|-----|-----|-----|-----|
| 0 | SC | SC | SC | SA | SA | SA | CP |
| 1 | SC | SC | SA | SA | SA | CP | CP |
| 2 | SC | SA | SA | CP | CP | CP | AQ |
| 3 | SA | SA | CP | CP | CP | AQ | AQ |
| 4 | SA | CP | CP | CP | AQ | AQ | PI |
| 5 | CP | CP | AQ | AQ | AQ | PI | PI |
| 6 | CP | AQ | AQ | AQ | AQ | PI | AR |
| 7 | AQ | AQ | PI | PI | PI | AR | AR |
| 8 | AQ | PI | PI | PI | PI | AR | AR |
| 9 | AQ | PI | PI | AR | AR | TA | TA |
| 10 | PI | AR | AR | AR | AR | TA | TA |
| 11 | PI | AR | AR | TA | TA | TA | GE |
| 12 | AR | TA | TA | TA | TA | GE | GE |
| 13 | AR | TA | TA | GE | GE | GE | GE |
| 14 | TA | GE | GE | GE | GE | CA | CA |
| 15 | TA | TA | TA | GE | GE | GE | CA |
| 16 | TA | GE | GE | GE | CA | CA | CA |
| 17 | GE | GE | GE | CA | CA | CA | LE |
| 18 | GE | GE | CA | CA | CA | LE | LE |
| 19 | GE | CA | CA | CA | LE | LE | LE |
| 20 | CA | CA | CA | LE | LE | LE | VI |
| 21 | CA | CA | LE | LE | LE | VI | VI |
| 22 | CA | LE | LE | VI | VI | VI | LI |
| 23 | LE | LE | LE | VI | VI | VI | LI |
| 24 | LE | LE | VI | VI | VI | LI | LI |
| 25 | LE | VI | VI | LI | LI | LI | SC |
| 26 | VI | VI | LI | LI | LI | SC | SC |
| 27 | VI | LI | LI | SC | SC | SC | SA |
| 28 | LI | LI | LI | SC | SC | SC | SA |
| 29 | LI | LI | SC | SC | SA | SA | SA |

AR = Aries, TA = Taurus, GE = Gemini, CA = Cancer, LE = Leo, VI = Virgo, LI = Libra, SC = Scorpio, SA = Sagittarius, CP = Capricorn, AQ = Aquarius, PI = Pisces

# MOON SIGNS

## Moon in Aries

You have a strong imagination, courage, determination and a desire to do things in your own way and forge your own path through life.

Originality is a key attribute; you are seldom stuck for ideas although your mind is changeable and you could take the time to focus on individual tasks. Often quick-tempered, you take orders from few people and live life at a fast pace. Avoid health problems by taking regular time out for rest and relaxation.

Emotionally, it is important that you talk to those you are closest to and work out your true feelings. Once you discover that people are there to help, there is less necessity for you to do everything yourself.

## Moon in Taurus

The Moon in Taurus gives you a courteous and friendly manner, which means you are likely to have many friends.

The good things in life mean a lot to you, as Taurus is an Earth sign that delights in experiences which please the senses. Hence you are probably a lover of good food and drink, which may in turn mean you need to keep an eye on the bathroom scales, especially as looking good is also important to you.

Emotionally you are fairly stable and you stick by your own standards. Taureans do not respond well to change. Intuition also plays an important part in your life.

## Moon in Gemini

You have a warm-hearted character, sympathetic and eager to help others. At times reserved, you can also be articulate and chatty: this is part of the paradox of Gemini, which always brings duplicity to the nature. You are interested in current affairs, have a good intellect, and are good company and likely to have many friends. Most of your friends have a high opinion of you and would be ready to defend you should the need arise. However, this is usually unnecessary, as you are quite capable of defending yourself in any verbal confrontation.

Travel is important to your inquisitive mind and you find intellectual stimulus in mixing with people from different cultures. You also gain much from reading, writing and the arts but you do need plenty of rest and relaxation in order to avoid fatigue.

## Moon in Cancer

The Moon in Cancer at the time of birth is a fortunate position as Cancer is the Moon's natural home. This means that the qualities of compassion and understanding given by the Moon are especially enhanced in your nature, and you are friendly and sociable and cope well with emotional pressures. You cherish home and family life, and happily do the domestic tasks. Your surroundings are important to you and you hate squalor and filth. You are likely to have a love of music and poetry.

Your basic character, although at times changeable like the Moon itself, depends on symmetry. You aim to make your surroundings comfortable and harmonious, for yourself and those close to you.

## Moon in Leo

The best qualities of the Moon and Leo come together to make you warmhearted, fair, ambitious and self-confident. With good organisational abilities, you invariably rise to a position of responsibility in your chosen career. This is fortunate as you don't enjoy being an 'also-ran' and would rather be an important part of a small organisation than a menial in a large one.

You should be lucky in love, and happy, provided you put in the effort to make a comfortable home for yourself and those close to you. It is likely that you will have a love of pleasure, sport, music and literature. Life brings you many rewards, most of them as a direct result of your own efforts, although you may be luckier than average and ready to make the best of any situation.

## Moon in Virgo

You are endowed with good mental abilities and a keen receptive memory, but you are never ostentatious or pretentious. Naturally quite reserved, you still have many friends, especially of the opposite sex. Marital relationships must be discussed carefully and worked at so that they remain harmonious, as personal attachments can be a problem if you do not give them your full attention.

Talented and persevering, you possess artistic qualities and are a good homemaker. Earning your honours through genuine merit, you work long and hard towards your objectives but show little pride in your achievements. Many short journeys will be undertaken in your life.

## Moon in Libra

With the Moon in Libra you are naturally popular and make friends easily. People like you, probably more than you realise, you bring fun to a party and are a natural diplomat. For all its good points, Libra is not the most stable of astrological signs and, as a result, your emotions can be a little unstable too. Therefore, although the Moon in Libra is said to be good for love and marriage, your Sun sign and Rising sign will have an important effect on your emotional and loving qualities.

You must remember to relate to others in your decision-making. Co-operation is crucial because Libra represents the 'balance' of life that can only be achieved through harmonious relationships. Conformity is not easy for you because Libra, an Air sign, likes its independence.

## Moon in Scorpio

Some people might call you pushy. In fact, all you really want to do is to live life to the full and protect yourself and your family from the pressures of life. Take care to avoid giving the impression of being sarcastic or impulsive and use your energies wisely and constructively.

You have great courage and you invariably achieve your goals by force of personality and sheer effort. You are fond of mystery and are good at predicting the outcome of situations and events. Travel experiences can be beneficial to you.

You may experience problems if you do not take time to examine your motives in a relationship, and also if you allow jealousy, always a feature of Scorpio, to cloud your judgement.

## Moon in Sagittarius

The Moon in Sagittarius helps to make you a generous individual with humanitarian qualities and a kind heart. Restlessness may be intrinsic as your mind is seldom still. Perhaps because of this, you have a need for change that could lead you to several major moves during your adult life. You are not afraid to stand your ground when you know your judgement is right, you speak directly and have good intuition.

At work you are quick, efficient and versatile and so you make an ideal employee. You need work to be intellectually demanding and do not enjoy tedious routines.

In relationships, you anger quickly if faced with stupidity or deception, though you are just as quick to forgive and forget. Emotionally, there are times when your heart rules your head.

## Moon in Capricorn

The Moon in Capricorn makes you popular and likely to come into the public eye in some way. The watery Moon is not entirely comfortable in the Earth sign of Capricorn and this may lead to some difficulties in the early years of life. An initial lack of creative ability and indecision must be overcome before the true qualities of patience and perseverance inherent in Capricorn can show through.

You have good administrative ability and are a capable worker, and if you are careful you can accumulate wealth. But you must be cautious and take professional advice in partnerships, as you are open to deception. You may be interested in social or welfare work, which suit your organisational skills and sympathy for others.

## Moon in Aquarius

The Moon in Aquarius makes you an active and agreeable person with a friendly, easy-going nature. Sympathetic to the needs of others, you flourish in a laid-back atmosphere. You are broad-minded, fair and open to suggestion, although sometimes you have an unconventional quality which others can find hard to understand.

You are interested in the strange and curious, and in old articles and places. You enjoy trips to these places and gain much from them. Political, scientific and educational work interests you and you might choose a career in science or technology.

Money-wise, you make gains through innovation and concentration and Lunar Aquarians often tackle more than one job at a time. In love you are kind and honest.

## Moon in Pisces

You have a kind, sympathetic nature, somewhat retiring at times, but you always take account of others' feelings and help when you can.

Personal relationships may be problematic, but as life goes on you can learn from your experiences and develop a better understanding of yourself and the world around you.

You have a fondness for travel, appreciate beauty and harmony and hate disorder and strife. You may be fond of literature and would make a good writer or speaker yourself. You have a creative imagination and may come across as an incurable romantic. You have strong intuition, maybe bordering on a mediumistic quality, which sets you apart from the mass. You may not be rich in cash terms, but your personal gifts are worth more than gold.

# SAGITTARIUS IN LOVE

**D**iscover how compatible in love you are with people from the same and other signs of the zodiac. Five stars equals a match made in heaven!

## Sagittarius meets Sagittarius

Although perhaps not the very best partnership for Sagittarius, this must rank as one of the most eventful, electrifying and interesting of the bunch. They will think alike, which is often the key to any relationship but, unfortunately, they may be so busy leading their own lives that they don't spend much time together. Their social life should be something special, and there could be lots of travel. However, domestic responsibilities need to be carefully shared and the family might benefit from a helping hand in this area. Star rating: ****

## Sagittarius meets Capricorn

Any real problem here will stem from a lack of understanding. Capricorn is very practical and needs to be constantly on the go, though in a fairly low-key sort of way. Sagittarius is busy too, though always in a panic and invariably behind its deadlines, which will annoy organised Capricorn. Sagittarius doesn't really have the depth of nature that best suits an Earth sign like Capricorn and its flirty nature could upset the sensitive Goat, though its lighter attitude could be cheering, too. Star rating: ***

## Sagittarius meets Aquarius

Both Sagittarius and Aquarius are into mind games, which may lead to something of an intellectual competition. If one side is happy to be bamboozled it won't be a problem, but it is more likely that the relationship will turn into a competition which won't auger well for its long-term future. However, on the plus side, both signs are adventurous and sociable, so as long as there is always something new and interesting to do, the match could end up turning out very well. Star rating: **

## Sagittarius meets Pisces

Probably the least likely success story for either sign, which is why it scores so low on the star rating. The basic problem is an almost total lack of understanding. A successful relationship needs empathy and progress towards a shared goal but, although both are eager to please, Pisces is too deep and Sagittarius too flighty – they just don't belong on the same planet! As pals, they have more in common and so a friendship is the best hope of success and happiness. Star rating: *

## Sagittarius meets Aries

This can be one of the most favourable matches of them all. Both Aries and Sagittarius are Fire signs, which often leads to clashes of will, but this pair find a mutual understanding. Sagittarius helps Aries to develop a better sense of humour, while Aries teaches the Archer about consistency on the road to success. Some patience is called for on both sides, but these people have a natural liking for each other. Add this to growing love and you have a long-lasting combination that is hard to beat. Star rating: *****

## Sagittarius meets Taurus

On first impression, Taurus may not like Sagittarius, which may seem brash, and even common, when viewed through the Bull's refined eyes. But, there is hope of success because the two signs have so much to offer each other. The Archer is enthralled by the Taurean's natural poise and beauty, while Taurus always needs more basic confidence, which is no problem to Sagittarius who has plenty to spare. Both signs love to travel. There are certain to be ups and downs, but that doesn't prevent an interesting, inspiring and even exciting combination. Star rating: ***

## Sagittarius meets Gemini

A paradoxical relationship this. On paper, the two signs have much in common, but unfortunately, they are often so alike that life turns into a fiercely fought competition. Both signs love change and diversity and both want to be the life and soul of the party. But in life there must always be a leader and a follower, and neither of this pair wants to be second. Both also share a tendency towards infidelity, which may develop into a problem as time passes. This could be an interesting match, but not necessarily successful. Star rating: **

## Sagittarius meets Cancer

Although probably not an immediate success, there is hope for this couple. It's hard to see how this pair could get together, because they have few mutual interests. Sagittarius is always on the go, loves a hectic social life and dances the night away. Cancer prefers the cinema or a concert. But, having met, Cancer will appreciate the Archer's happy and cheerful nature, while Sagittarius finds Cancer alluring and intriguing and, as the saying goes, opposites attract. A long-term relationship would focus on commitment to family, with Cancer leading this area. Star rating: ***

## Sagittarius meets Leo

An excellent match as Leo and Sagittarius have so much in common. Their general approach to life is very similar, although as they are both Fire signs they can clash impressively! Sagittarius is shallower and more flippant than Leo likes to think of itself, and the Archer will be the one taking emotional chances. Sagittarius has met its match in the Lion's den, as brave Leo won't be outdone by anyone. Financially, they will either be very wealthy or struggling, and family life may be chaotic. Problems, like joys, are handled jointly – and that leads to happiness. Star rating: *****

## Sagittarius meets Virgo

There can be some quite strange happenings inside this relationship. Sagittarius and Virgo view life so differently there are always new discoveries. Virgo is much more of a home-bird than Sagittarius, but that won't matter if the Archer introduces its hectic social life gradually. More importantly, Sagittarius understands that it takes Virgo a long time to free its hidden 'inner sprite', but once free it will be fun all the way – until Virgo's thrifty nature takes over. There are great possibilities, but effort is required. Star rating: ***

## Sagittarius meets Libra

Libra and Sagittarius are both adaptable signs who get on well with most people, but this promising outlook often does not follow through because each brings out the 'flighty' side of the other. This combination is great for a fling, but when the romance is over someone needs to see to the practical side of life. Both signs are well meaning, pleasant and kind, but are either of them constant enough to build a life together? In at least some cases, the answer would be no. Star rating: ***

## Sagittarius meets Scorpio

Sagittarius needs constant stimulation and loves to be busy from dawn till dusk which may mean that it feels rather frustrated by Scorpio. Scorpions are hard workers, too, but they are also contemplative and need periods of quiet which may mean that they appear dull to Sagittarius. This could lead to a gulf between the two which must be overcome. With time and patience on both sides, this can be a lucrative encounter and good in terms of home and family. A variable alliance. Star rating: ***

# VENUS:
# THE PLANET OF LOVE

If you look up at the sky around sunset or sunrise you will often see Venus in close attendance to the Sun. It is arguably one of the most beautiful sights of all and there is little wonder that historically it became associated with the goddess of love. But although Venus does play an important part in the way you view love and in the way others see you romantically, this is only one of the spheres of influence that it enjoys in your overall character.

Venus has a part to play in the more cultured side of your life and has much to do with your appreciation of art, literature, music and general creativity. Even the way you look is responsive to the part of the zodiac that Venus occupied at the start of your life, though this fact is also down to your Sun sign and Ascending sign. If, at the time you were born, Venus occupied one of the more gregarious zodiac signs, you will be more likely to wear your heart on your sleeve, as well as to be more attracted to entertainment, social gatherings and good company. If on the other hand Venus occupied a quiet zodiac sign at the time of your birth, you would tend to be more retiring and less willing to shine in public situations.

It's good to know what part the planet Venus plays in your life, for it can have a great bearing on the way you appear to the rest of the world and since we all have to mix with others, you can learn to make the very best of what Venus has to offer you.

One of the great complications in the past has always been trying to establish exactly what zodiac position Venus enjoyed when you were born, because the planet is notoriously difficult to track. However, I have solved that problem by creating a table that is exclusive to your Sun sign, which you will find on the following page.

Establishing your Venus sign could not be easier. Just look up the year of your birth on the page opposite and you will see a sign of the zodiac. This was the sign that Venus occupied in the period covered by your sign in that year. If Venus occupied more than one sign during the period, this is indicated by the date on which the sign changed, and the name of the new sign. For instance, if you were born in 1950, Venus was in Sagittarius until the 16th December, after which time it was in Capricorn. If you were born before 16th December your Venus sign is Sagittarius, if you were born on or after 16th December, your Venus sign is Capricorn. Once you have established the position of Venus at the time of your birth, you can then look in the pages which follow to see how this has a bearing on your life as a whole.

1919 LIBRA / 9.12 SCORPIO
1920 CAPRICORN / 13.12 AQUARIUS
1921 SCORPIO / 7.12 SAGITTARIUS
1922 SAGITTARIUS / 29.11 SCORPIO
1923 SAGITTARIUS / 2.12 CAPRICORN
1924 LIBRA / 27.11 SCORPIO
1925 CAPRICORN / 6.12 AQUARIUS
1926 SAGITTARIUS / 17.12 CAPRICORN
1927 LIBRA / 9.12 SCORPIO
1928 CAPRICORN / 13.12 AQUARIUS
1929 SCORPIO / 7.12 SAGITTARIUS
1930 SCORPIO
1931 SAGITTARIUS / 2.12 CAPRICORN
1932 LIBRA / 26.11 SCORPIO
1933 CAPRICORN / 6.12 AQUARIUS
1934 SAGITTARIUS / 17.12 CAPRICORN
1935 LIBRA / 10.12 SCORPIO
1936 CAPRICORN / 12.12 AQUARIUS
1937 SCORPIO / 6.12 SAGITTARIUS
1938 SCORPIO
1939 SAGITTARIUS / 1.12 CAPRICORN
1940 LIBRA / 26.11 SCORPIO
1941 CAPRICORN / 6.12 AQUARIUS
1942 SAGITTARIUS / 16.12 CAPRICORN
1943 LIBRA / 10.12 SCORPIO
1944 CAPRICORN / 12.12 AQUARIUS
1945 SCORPIO / 6.12 SAGITTARIUS
1946 SCORPIO
1947 SAGITTARIUS / 1.12 CAPRICORN
1948 LIBRA / 25.11 SCORPIO /
    20.12 SAGITTARIUS
1949 CAPRICORN / 7.12 AQUARIUS
1950 SAGITTARIUS / 16.12 CAPRICORN
1951 LIBRA / 10.12 SCORPIO
1952 CAPRICORN / 11.12 AQUARIUS
1953 SCORPIO / 5.12 SAGITTARIUS
1954 SCORPIO
1955 SAGITTARIUS / 30.11 CAPRICORN
1956 LIBRA / 25.11 SCORPIO /
    20.12 SAGITTARIUS
1957 CAPRICORN / 8.12 AQUARIUS
1958 SAGITTARIUS / 15.12 CAPRICORN
1959 LIBRA / 10.12 SCORPIO
1960 CAPRICORN / 11.12 AQUARIUS
1961 SCORPIO / 5.12 SAGITTARIUS
1962 SCORPIO
1963 SAGITTARIUS / 30.11 CAPRICORN
1964 LIBRA / 24.11 SCORPIO /
    19.12 SAGITTARIUS
1965 CAPRICORN / 8.12 AQUARIUS
1966 SAGITTARIUS / 15.12 CAPRICORN
1967 LIBRA / 10.12 SCORPIO
1968 CAPRICORN / 10.12 AQUARIUS

1969 SCORPIO / 4.12 SAGITTARIUS
1970 SCORPIO
1971 SAGITTARIUS / 29.11 CAPRICORN
1972 LIBRA / 24.11 SCORPIO /
    19.12 SAGITTARIUS
1973 CAPRICORN / 9.12 AQUARIUS
1974 SAGITTARIUS / 14.12 CAPRICORN
1975 LIBRA / 9.12 SCORPIO
1976 CAPRICORN / 9.12 AQUARIUS
1977 SCORPIO / 4.12 SAGITTARIUS
1978 SCORPIO
1979 SAGITTARIUS / 28.11 CAPRICORN
1980 SCORPIO / 18.12 SAGITTARIUS
1981 CAPRICORN / 10.12 AQUARIUS
1982 SAGITTARIUS / 14.12 CAPRICORN
1983 LIBRA / 9.12 SCORPIO
1984 CAPRICORN / 9.12 AQUARIUS
1985 SCORPIO / 3.12 SAGITTARIUS
1986 SCORPIO
1987 SAGITTARIUS / 28.11 CAPRICORN
1988 SCORPIO / 18.12 SAGITTARIUS
1989 CAPRICORN / 11.12 AQUARIUS
1990 SAGITTARIUS / 13.12 CAPRICORN
1991 LIBRA / 9.12 SCORPIO
1992 CAPRICORN / 9.12 AQUARIUS
1993 SCORPIO / 3.12 SAGITTARIUS
1994 SCORPIO
1995 SAGITTARIUS / 28.11 CAPRICORN
1996 SCORPIO / 17.12 SAGITTARIUS
1997 CAPRICORN / 12.12 AQUARIUS
1998 SAGITTARIUS / 13.12 CAPRICORN
1999 LIBRA / 9.12 SCORPIO
2000 CAPRICORN / 8.12 AQUARIUS
2001 SCORPIO / 3.12 SAGITTARIUS
2002 SCORPIO
2003 SAGITTARIUS / 28.11 CAPRICORN
2004 SCORPIO / 17.12 SAGITTARIUS
2005 CAPRICORN / 12.12 AQUARIUS
2006 SAGITTARIUS / 13.12 CAPRICORN
2007 LIBRA / 9.12 SCORPIO
2008 CAPRICORN / 8.12 AQUARIUS
2009 SCORPIO / 3.12 AQUARIUS
2010 SCORPIO
2011 SAGITTARIUS / 28.11 CAPRICORN
2012 SCORPIO / 17.12 SAGITTARIUS
2013 SAGITTARIUS / 13.12 CAPRICORN
2014 SAGITTARIUS / 13.12 CAPRICORN
2015 LIBRA / 9.12 SCORPIO
2016 CAPRICORN / 8.12 AQUARIUS
2017 SCORPIO / 3.12 AQUARIUS

# VENUS THROUGH THE ZODIAC SIGNS

## Venus in Aries

Amongst other things, the position of Venus in Aries indicates a fondness for travel, music and all creative pursuits. Your nature tends to be affectionate and you would try not to create confusion or difficulty for others if it could be avoided. Many people with this planetary position have a great love of the theatre, and mental stimulation is of the greatest importance. Early romantic attachments are common with Venus in Aries, so it is very important to establish a genuine sense of romantic continuity. Early marriage is not recommended, especially if it is based on sympathy. You may give your heart a little too readily on occasions.

## Venus in Taurus

You are capable of very deep feelings and your emotions tend to last for a very long time. This makes you a trusting partner and lover, whose constancy is second to none. In life you are precise and careful and always try to do things the right way. Although this means an ordered life, which you are comfortable with, it can also lead you to be rather too fussy for your own good. Despite your pleasant nature, you are very fixed in your opinions and quite able to speak your mind. Others are attracted to you and historical astrologers always quoted this position of Venus as being very fortunate in terms of marriage. However, if you find yourself involved in a failed relationship, it could take you a long time to trust again.

## Venus in Gemini

As with all associations related to Gemini, you tend to be quite versatile, anxious for change and intelligent in your dealings with the world at large. You may gain money from more than one source but you are equally good at spending it. There is an inference here that you are a good communicator, via either the written or the spoken word, and you love to be in the company of interesting people. Always on the look-out for culture, you may also be very fond of music, and love to indulge the curious and cultured side of your nature. In romance you tend to have more than one relationship and could find yourself associated with someone who has previously been a friend or even a distant relative.

## Venus in Cancer

You often stay close to home because you are very fond of family and enjoy many of your most treasured moments when you are with those you love. Being naturally sympathetic, you will always do anything you can to support those around you, even people you hardly know at all. This charitable side of your nature is your most noticeable trait and is one of the reasons why others are naturally so fond of you. Being receptive and in some cases even psychic, you can see through to the soul of most of those with whom you come into contact. You may not commence too many romantic attachments but when you do give your heart, it tends to be unconditionally.

## Venus in Leo

It must become quickly obvious to almost anyone you meet that you are kind, sympathetic and yet determined enough to stand up for anyone or anything that is truly important to you. Bright and sunny, you warm the world with your natural enthusiasm and would rarely do anything to hurt those around you, or at least not intentionally. In romance you are ardent and sincere, though some may find your style just a little overpowering. Gains come through your contacts with other people and this could be especially true with regard to romance, for love and money often come hand in hand for those who were born with Venus in Leo. People claim to understand you, though you are more complex than you seem.

## Venus in Virgo

Your nature could well be fairly quiet no matter what your Sun sign might be, though this fact often manifests itself as an inner peace and would not prevent you from being basically sociable. Some delays and even the odd disappointment in love cannot be ruled out with this planetary position, though it's a fact that you will usually find the happiness you look for in the end. Catapulting yourself into romantic entanglements that you know to be rather ill-advised is not sensible, and it would be better to wait before you committed yourself exclusively to any one person. It is the essence of your nature to serve the world at large and through doing so it is possible that you will attract money at some stage in your life.

## Venus in Libra

Venus is very comfortable in Libra and bestows upon those people who have this planetary position a particular sort of kindness that is easy to recognise. This is a very good position for all sorts of friendships and also for romantic attachments that usually bring much joy into your life. Few individuals with Venus in Libra would avoid marriage and since you are capable of great depths of love, it is likely that you will find a contented personal life. You like to mix with people of integrity and intelligence but don't take kindly to scruffy surroundings or work that means getting your hands too dirty. Careful speculation, good business dealings and money through marriage all seem fairly likely.

## Venus in Scorpio

You are quite open and tend to spend money quite freely, even on those occasions when you don't have very much. Although your intentions are always good, there are times when you get yourself in to the odd scrape and this can be particularly true when it comes to romance, which you may come to late or from a rather unexpected direction. Certainly you have the power to be happy and to make others contented on the way, but you find the odd stumbling block on your journey through life and it could seem that you have to work harder than those around you. As a result of this, you gain a much deeper understanding of the true value of personal happiness than many people ever do, and are likely to achieve true contentment in the end.

## Venus in Sagittarius

You are lighthearted, cheerful and always able to see the funny side of any situation. These facts enhance your popularity, which is especially high with members of the opposite sex. You should never have to look too far to find romantic interest in your life, though it is just possible that you might be too willing to commit yourself before you are certain that the person in question is right for you. Part of the problem here extends to other areas of life too. The fact is that you like variety in everything and so can tire of situations that fail to offer it. All the same, if you choose wisely and learn to understand your restless side, then great happiness can be yours.

## Venus in Capricorn

The most notable trait that comes from Venus in this position is that it makes you trustworthy and able to take on all sorts of responsibilities in life. People are instinctively fond of you and love you all the more because you are always ready to help those who are in any form of need. Social and business popularity can be yours and there is a magnetic quality to your nature that is particularly attractive in a romantic sense. Anyone who wants a partner for a lover, a spouse and a good friend too would almost certainly look in your direction. Constancy is the hallmark of your nature and unfaithfulness would go right against the grain. You might sometimes be a little too trusting.

## Venus in Aquarius

This location of Venus offers a fondness for travel and a desire to try out something new at every possible opportunity. You are extremely easy to get along with and tend to have many friends from varied backgrounds, classes and inclinations. You like to live a distinct sort of life and gain a great deal from moving about, both in a career sense and with regard to your home. It is not out of the question that you could form a romantic attachment to someone who comes from far away or be attracted to a person of a distinctly artistic and original nature. What you cannot stand is jealousy, for you have friends of both sexes and would want to keep things that way.

## Venus in Pisces

The first thing people tend to notice about you is your wonderful, warm smile. Being very charitable by nature you will do anything to help others, even if you don't know them well. Much of your life may be spent sorting out situations for other people, but it is very important to feel that you are living for yourself too. In the main, you remain cheerful, and tend to be quite attractive to members of the opposite sex. Where romantic attachments are concerned, you could be drawn to people who are significantly older or younger than yourself or to someone with a unique career or point of view. It might be best for you to avoid marrying whilst you are still very young.

# HOW THE DIAGRAMS WORK

Through the picture diagrams in the Astral Diary I want to help you to plot your year. With them you can see where the positive and negative aspects will be found in each month. To make the most of them, all you have to do is remember where and when!

Let me show you how they work ...

## THE MONTH AT A GLANCE

Just as there are twelve separate zodiac signs, so astrologers believe that each sign has twelve separate aspects to life. Each of the twelve segments relates to a different personal aspect. I list them all every month so that their meanings are always clear.

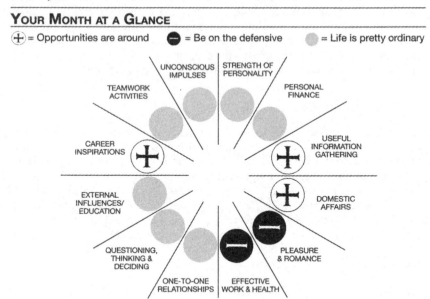

YOUR MONTH AT A GLANCE

+ = Opportunities are around    − = Be on the defensive    = Life is pretty ordinary

UNCONSCIOUS IMPULSES

STRENGTH OF PERSONALITY

TEAMWORK ACTIVITIES

PERSONAL FINANCE

CAREER INSPIRATIONS

USEFUL INFORMATION GATHERING

EXTERNAL INFLUENCES/ EDUCATION

DOMESTIC AFFAIRS

QUESTIONING, THINKING & DECIDING

PLEASURE & ROMANCE

ONE-TO-ONE RELATIONSHIPS

EFFECTIVE WORK & HEALTH

I have designed this chart to show you how and when these twelve different aspects are being influenced throughout the year. When there is a shaded circle, nothing out of the ordinary is to be expected. However, when a circle turns white with a plus sign, the influence is positive. Where the circle is black with a minus sign, it is a negative.

## YOUR ENERGY RHYTHM CHART

Below is a picture diagram in which I link your zodiac group to the rhythm of the Moon. In doing this I have calculated when you will be gaining strength from its influence and equally when you may be weakened by it.

If you think of yourself as being like the tides of the ocean then you may understand how your own energies must also rise and fall. And if you understand how it works and when it is working, then you can better organise your activities to achieve more and get things done more easily.

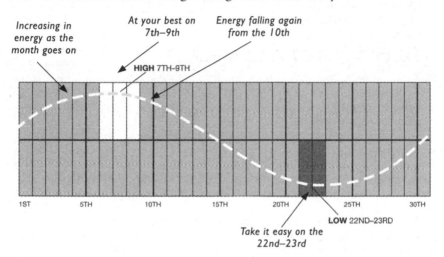

## THE KEY DAYS

Some of the entries are in **bold**, which indicates the working of astrological cycles in your life. Look out for them each week as they are the best days to take action or make decisions. The daily text tells you which area of your life to focus on.

## MERCURY RETROGRADE

The Mercury symbol (☿) indicates that Mercury is retrograde on that day. Since Mercury governs communication, the fact that it appears to be moving backwards when viewed from the Earth at this time should warn you that your communication skills are not likely to be at their best and you could expect some setbacks.

# SAGITTARIUS: YOUR YEAR IN BRIEF

With a new year comes all sorts of possibilities. In a positive frame of mind, now you may want to tackle things that have been on the back burner for quite some. Both January and February indicate the start of a progressive phase with the chance of a little extra cash coming your way. Don't allow yourself to get into any sort of rut and do what you can to bring variety into your life.

The early spring months of March and April should find you anxious to get on with things, even when other people are more reticent. There are financial gains to be made, especially during March, with April then bringing a period of consolidation. Routines won't appeal to you much at this time but you will remain very practical in most situations. The bright and breezy side of your nature is clearly on display.

May and June bring the early summer and should both be months of significant movement and activity. There are gains to be made in matters of love, with new relationships cropping up for some Archers and plenty of chance to show just what a social animal you are. June in particular could bring some lucky breaks when it comes to making more money, and some Sagittarians may make a whole new start.

July and August bring their own benefits and these should become more or less immediately obvious. There are gains to be made as a result of past and present efforts, as well as through the involvement in your life of new people or those you haven't seen for quite some time. Throughout most of this period you will be active and anxious to score a number of successes. These appear in various different areas of your life.

As the summer draws to a close, September and October find you bringing things together and integrating certain areas of your life more than was possible earlier in the year. You are likely to be fairly satisfied with your overall progress and keen to put it on a firm and secure footing. Trends also suggest the chance of some long-distance travel. Business as well as social trends look especially good during October.

The last two months of the year, November and December, will see you less active and enterprising, especially at the very end of the year and somewhat unwilling to go that extra mile, as was the case in the summer months. A more conservative attitude is possible, especially in December, and consolidation is the key. By the Christmas period you will gain a little more momentum and, as is frequently the case for you, it looks as though you will be putting yourself out so that others can enjoy themselves more.

2017

## YOUR MONTH AT A GLANCE

⊕ = Opportunities are around  ⊖ = Be on the defensive  ⬤ = Life is pretty ordinary

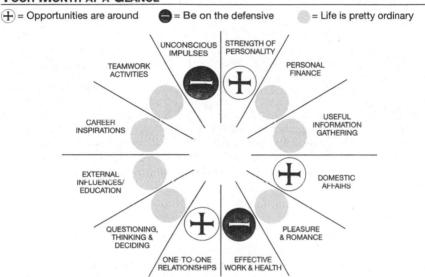

## JANUARY HIGHS AND LOWS

*Here I show you how the rhythms of the Moon will affect you this month. Like the tide, your energies and abilities will rise and fall with its pattern. When it is above the centre line, go for it, when it is below, you should be resting.*

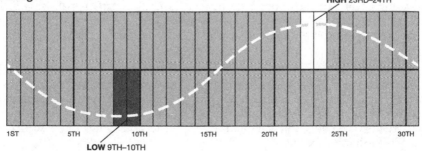

**HIGH** 23RD–24TH

**LOW** 9TH–10TH

45

## I SUNDAY ☿ *Moon Age Day 4    Moon Sign Aquarius*

As the new year dawns, you should be in the mood to talk to influential people. There is certainly a chance that this might lead to some important gains as the month advances. Life may not be going all your own way but in a romantic sense things are likely to work out well. There are distinct advantages to the way Sagittarius looks at things right now.

## 2 MONDAY ☿ *Moon Age Day 5    Moon Sign Aquarius*

This is a time to be taking calculated risks, especially at work. Of course you won't want to put your safety on the line but the odd chance when it comes to your contact with superiors or those in a position of influence could work out well. Your confidence to say and do the right thing remains essentially strong, which should help you to avoid blunders.

## 3 TUESDAY ☿ *Moon Age Day 6    Moon Sign Pisces*

There is a lot of energy behind almost everything you either think or say today. This isn't unusual for Sagittarius but what is slightly different is that your efforts are more concentrated and effective. It is important to be selective now if you want to make the very best impression on the world at large.

## 4 WEDNESDAY ☿ *Moon Age Day 7    Moon Sign Pisces*

Focus on your finances today and try to devise some sort of cohesive plan for the future. You might be slightly luckier now than of late and will certainly have what it takes to see the bigger picture. Friends are likely to be very supportive and will most probably find you particularly attractive and good company now.

## 5 THURSDAY ☿ *Moon Age Day 8    Moon Sign Aries*

There is plenty to keep you fairly happy and busily on the go. All the same, it's important to organise your personal schedule as carefully as you can if you don't want to start confusing issues. Some Sagittarians will be a little absentminded today, so write things down and keep a close eye on your work diary and home commitments.

## 6 FRIDAY ☿ *Moon Age Day 9    Moon Sign Aries*

This looks likely to be a fairly good period in terms of finances and a time during which you can consolidate your position and even move forward somewhat. This hasn't necessarily been the case over the last few months, but trends that begin today should leave you feeling rather more secure in the weeks that lie ahead.

## 7 SATURDAY ☿ *Moon Age Day 10  Moon Sign Taurus*

Look out for gifts of appreciation, doubtless coming from those who have very good reason to thank you for your efforts on their behalf. The weekend is here, which is good because a change of scenery would do you a great deal of good at the moment. Although it is still the middle of the winter, you are restless and in need of some amusement.

## 8 SUNDAY *Moon Age Day 11  Moon Sign Taurus*

You desire freedom at almost any cost and that can get you into some slight trouble if you are not careful. It would be better if you looked ahead cautiously but this is the last thing you are likely to be doing right now. People you don't see very often might be the ones to offer you the soundest advice and it would be sensible to at least listen to them.

## 9 MONDAY *Moon Age Day 12  Moon Sign Gemini*

Just slow down the decision making for a day or two. The monthly lunar low comes along as the Moon enters your opposite sign of Gemini and this makes it all the more likely that you will trip over your own feet. It would be a shame to spoil weeks or months of careful planning through some hasty action now. If you have to settle for second best, it won't be for very long.

## 10 TUESDAY *Moon Age Day 13  Moon Sign Gemini*

Your strength is limited, as is your ability to move forward as progressively as you generally want to. At least this offers you the chance to look around and to take a breather. Romantically speaking, you remain extremely attractive, although there is a chance that this could extend to someone whose attachment to you could be embarrassing.

## 11 WEDNESDAY *Moon Age Day 14  Moon Sign Cancer*

Rash or impulsive actions can prove to be quite self-defeating, which is why you should move forward slowly and steadily at present. What is required is positive and concerted effort and there is no reason at all for you to rush things. Friends might be willing to lend a hand but you may be slightly reluctant to accept.

## 12 THURSDAY *Moon Age Day 15  Moon Sign Cancer*

You have an opportunity to make money now but is the incentive to do so really present? There are times during which the material things of life don't have quite as much appeal as they do on other occasions. You may indeed be looking beyond immediate monetary gains now, towards a more spiritual happiness.

## 13 FRIDAY
*Moon Age Day 16    Moon Sign Cancer*

Don't do too much dreaming today. Finding the right balance between thoughts and actions is certainly not easy at the moment but when life gets too simple you become bored. There should be some entertaining opportunities offered by life itself but if these do not present themselves you won't be afraid to make up your own adventure.

## 14 SATURDAY
*Moon Age Day 17    Moon Sign Leo*

Don't be in too much of a rush to achieve all your material objectives, if only because you need to save some possibilities for later. Spend a few hours enjoying what is around you now and mix as freely as you can with relatives and friends alike. For a few hours you can afford to genuinely relax.

## 15 SUNDAY
*Moon Age Day 18    Moon Sign Leo*

This is a good time for social groups and for getting to grips with issues that have been waiting around for some time. Your confidence grows significantly as you realise that much of your effort towards the end of last year is now beginning to pay dividends. Routines can be boring so change them if you can, or delegate them if you can't.

## 16 MONDAY
*Moon Age Day 19    Moon Sign Virgo*

Trends suggest that you might take up a new hobby now, especially since the winter weather means you cannot get out and about as much as you might wish. Creatively speaking, you are on top form, so there is no reason to avoid be held back. Be aware that unforced errors could creep into some of your efforts and check things thoroughly.

## 17 TUESDAY
*Moon Age Day 20    Moon Sign Virgo*

Rules and regulations are not always easy to follow now and you will tend to kick against at least some of them, especially if you know them to be plainly ridiculous. By all means work hard to stay ahead in certain respects but don't keep driving forward simply for the sake of doing so.

## 18 WEDNESDAY
*Moon Age Day 21    Moon Sign Libra*

You are keen to enjoy whatever life has to offer now, which might be a great deal. Socially speaking life is likely to be very good and you have few worries to hold you back. There is just a vague possibility that personal relationships are not everything they might be. Focus on the good things and everything else should come right soon.

## 19 THURSDAY

All of a sudden, there seems to be tons to get done and very little time in which to do it. If anyone can manage, Sagittarius can. Don't allow yourself to be restricted by colleagues who have doubts about your reasoning. The sort of jobs you are undertaking at the moment can only be resolved on the hoof.

## 20 FRIDAY

Your confidence is steady, but won't have been helped by a number of doubts that are circulating at present. There is a suggestion that you might be feeling apprehensive, or overly inclined to see problems in front of you. A naturally suspicious mind is not usually for you, so put this down to a blip and dismiss it out of hand.

## 21 SATURDAY

The weekend finds you anxious to have fun. The joking side of your nature is much in evidence and although you might tend to burn the candle at both ends today, yours is a zodiac sign that can get away with doing so. Bear in mind that there are some tasks that will benefit from being left alone and looked at again later.

## 22 SUNDAY

It appears that fun and games are the order of the day, mainly because you are in such a happy frame of mind. Even people who normally irritate you are less likely than usual to cause you any concern today and you should also be able to deal with issues that have been of some concern recently and put problems behind you.

## 23 MONDAY

**The Moon returns to your zodiac sign, bringing that two-day period known as the lunar high. You will have a very positive attitude to life generally and should be getting on very successfully with practical matters. Personal attachments and relationships also receive a significant positive boost around this time.**

## 24 TUESDAY

**This is another potentially good day and a period during which practically everything you have to say finds its mark. The Archer is firing off arrows in every direction and the world sits up and takes notice of your presence. Plans for the short-term future receive a significant boost thanks to the presence of attentive friends.**

## 25 WEDNESDAY
*Moon Age Day 28    Moon Sign Capricorn*

The Sun has now moved into your solar third house, which brings very positive highlights in terms of meetings, discussions and appointments. The way forward seems quite clear and your mind is working well. There won't be much doubt across the coming days regarding your charm and this heightens your ability to get what you want.

## 26 THURSDAY
*Moon Age Day 29    Moon Sign Capricorn*

There is a slight tendency to feel that it's just more of the same today and if so boredom is likely to set in. For Sagittarius to be happy, it is necessary to ring the changes regularly and take positive action on new initiatives. If you can't do this for some reason today, you can at least allow your mind to wander a little instead.

## 27 FRIDAY
*Moon Age Day 0    Moon Sign Capricorn*

Allow yourself some time off, particularly if you have been loading yourself down with masses of details, most of which are unimportant in the great scheme of things. With the weekend in view, you should be planning what comes next in a social sense. Be aware that family members may have an increased need of you today.

## 28 SATURDAY
*Moon Age Day 1    Moon Sign Aquarius*

Your level of patience tends to be lower than usual, particularly if people are pestering you for any reason. For example, you wouldn't take kindly to cold-callers or people knocking on the door and trying to sell you something. In a very real sense, you wish to be left alone today. As this is the weekend, you should be able to indulge these feelings for a day.

## 29 SUNDAY
*Moon Age Day 2    Moon Sign Aquarius*

Try to avoid situations in which it seems as though you are chasing your tail. Maybe some of the things you are pushing to get done are not actually all that urgent and in actual fact you would benefit more from some relaxation in order to reduce the stress you have been feeling. This is almost a constant problem for Sagittarius.

## 30 MONDAY
*Moon Age Day 3    Moon Sign Pisces*

Standing up for others is part of what this Monday is about. Brave and even a little foolhardy, you take on some of the bullies in life that others leave alone. Sagittarius is a natural street fighter, though fortunately only generally in a verbal sense. What you won't stand for today is any nonsense.

## 31 TUESDAY

Anything old or unusual in inclined to captivate your interest now, leading to some sort of personal investigation. It is true that part of your mind is now inclined to dwell in the past and you will find yourself looking back as much as forward. This is unlike Sagittarius and turns out to be a very temporary trend.

# *February*

2017

## YOUR MONTH AT A GLANCE

$+$ = Opportunities are around    $-$ = Be on the defensive    = Life is pretty ordinary

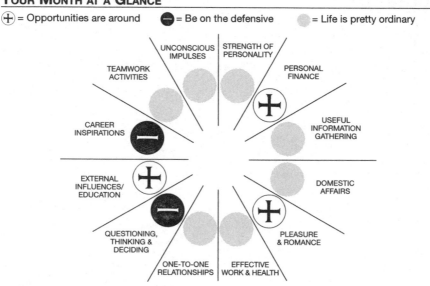

- UNCONSCIOUS IMPULSES
- STRENGTH OF PERSONALITY
- TEAMWORK ACTIVITIES
- PERSONAL FINANCE
- CAREER INSPIRATIONS
- USEFUL INFORMATION GATHERING
- EXTERNAL INFLUENCES/ EDUCATION
- DOMESTIC AFFAIRS
- QUESTIONING, THINKING & DECIDING
- PLEASURE & ROMANCE
- ONE-TO-ONE RELATIONSHIPS
- EFFECTIVE WORK & HEALTH

## FEBRUARY HIGHS AND LOWS

*Here I show you how the rhythms of the Moon will affect you this month. Like the tide, your energies and abilities will rise and fall with its pattern. When it is above the centre line, go for it, when it is below, you should be resting.*

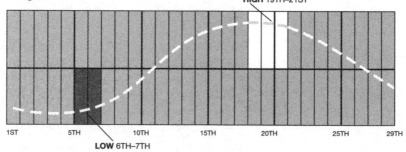

HIGH 19TH–21ST

1ST    5TH    10TH    15TH    20TH    25TH    29TH

LOW 6TH–7TH

## 1 WEDNESDAY
*Moon Age Day 5    Moon Sign Aries*

Family issues could cause you to worry a little more than might be necessary today. Of course such matters will have to be dealt with but you should not allow them to divert you from your own practical progress, something that is also on your mind at the moment. Listen to the sound advice of people you know well and trust.

## 2 THURSDAY
*Moon Age Day 6    Moon Sign Aries*

Now is a really good time to think about employing new strategies and for taking the initiative. This might not seem particularly easy to achieve when there is clearly opposition to some of your actions around but you will be surprised at just how much headway you are able to make. Find a way to spoil yourself by the evening.

## 3 FRIDAY
*Moon Age Day 7    Moon Sign Aries*

This is an ideal time for catching sight of problems before they mature. Damage-limitation exercises can then be put into place, avoiding further difficulties in the near future. You are able to act almost instantly and effectively and as a consequence will rise in the estimation of certain people who it is important to have on your side.

## 4 SATURDAY
*Moon Age Day 8    Moon Sign Taurus*

Maybe you notice the first breath of spring in the air this Saturday, which could lead to a determination on your part to ring the changes. You should avoid sitting around and becoming bored at any costs, and also the nagging feeling that your life is not going quite as you would wish. Stay flexible and keep on the move and a positive attitude will prevail.

## 5 SUNDAY
*Moon Age Day 9    Moon Sign Taurus*

Stick around familiar faces and places, at least for the moment. You still won't be very inclined today to take chances, and in any case your personal life is going to demand much of your time. With plenty to plan for, if not actually to do, you won't be short of places to turn your mind and some careful thought could stand you in good stead later.

## 6 MONDAY
*Moon Age Day 10    Moon Sign Gemini*

Now the Moon is in your opposite zodiac sign, which could slow things down quite noticeably. Don't be too quick to jump to conclusions and be prepared to leave tasks until later if you know you are not in the right frame of mind to be taking them on. There is no shame either in asking for assistance.

## 7 TUESDAY
*Moon Age Day 11    Moon Sign Gemini*

You are still not likely to be on top form but that doesn't mean you fail to enjoy yourself. Stick to things you know and associate with people who have always brought out the best in you. People you haven't seen for quite some time could appear in your world again very soon and you should make the most of them if they do.

## 8 WEDNESDAY
*Moon Age Day 12    Moon Sign Cancer*

Trends suggest that you are in the mood to do things your own way. That doesn't mean that you are withdrawing from others in a social sense. Some might say that on these occasions it might be better to stick to your own company, but this is unlikely to be the case for you. The Archer is nearly always a party animal.

## 9 THURSDAY
*Moon Age Day 13    Moon Sign Cancer*

Those in your home environment should be quite supportive at present and it is possible that around friends and family is where you will choose to be as much as possible today. You will be quite happy to get away from the cut and thrust of the practical world, if only for a short while.

## 10 FRIDAY
*Moon Age Day 14    Moon Sign Leo*

You now find opportunities that allow you to improve your domestic conditions and also relationships. The Archer is likely to be in the mood for romance and there are chances today to prove this to your spouse or partner. Your overtures should be well received but make sure you have your target right.

## 11 SATURDAY
*Moon Age Day 15    Moon Sign Leo*

Look out for a relaxing sort of day, with plenty to divert you from the material considerations of life. You would probably enjoy spending time with friends and since you are so very sociable at the moment, they in turn will relish the hours they spend with you. Today is about fun and not responsibility.

## 12 SUNDAY
*Moon Age Day 16    Moon Sign Virgo*

You are definitely at your best whilst amongst close friends, doing something that is both diverting and potentially useful. Mixing business with pleasure can be part of what this Sunday is about but this doesn't absolutely have to be the case. The main thing is that you find ways in which to amuse yourself and others.

## 13 MONDAY
*Moon Age Day 17    Moon Sign Virgo*

Some of those you meet today might seem quite critical. If the people who are pulling you up in your tracks are not the sort of people to cross you as a rule, accept that they may have a valid point. Sagittarius can be very determined and certainly pushy, but that doesn't mean to say you are always right. Take stock of the situation.

## 14 TUESDAY
*Moon Age Day 18    Moon Sign Libra*

You are anxious to be out there in the social mainstream, picking up useful information along the way and actively choosing to mix business with pleasure. Someone might try to throw a spanner in the works for you but chances are you got out of bed too early to allow such a thing and nothing should hold you back today.

## 15 WEDNESDAY
*Moon Age Day 19    Moon Sign Libra*

There is suddenly a strong emphasis on personal security, together tendency to look after 'me' and 'mine' that seems to have come like a bolt from the blue. The fact is that you are somewhat lacking in confidence today, maybe as a result of a casual word spoken by someone who didn't intend to stir up worries for you.

## 16 THURSDAY
*Moon Age Day 20    Moon Sign Libra*

Don't be afraid to reach out for what you want in life with both hands today. Although you could feel there are a number of small stumbling blocks to deal with at the moment, these should be sorted quickly, leaving much of the day as a tapestry on which you can put almost any design that comes into your head.

## 17 FRIDAY
*Moon Age Day 21    Moon Sign Scorpio*

Avoid arguments at home by keeping away from the people who seem to want to start them. You should be well organised in a practical sense and if there is any plan you have been waiting some time to put into action, today could be ideal. Conforming to the expectations that others have of you may not be very easy, though.

## 18 SATURDAY
*Moon Age Day 22    Moon Sign Scorpio*

Life seems to be filled with people of genuine personality this weekend. This isn't so surprising because you attract such people like iron filings to a magnet. You may feel the need for change and diversity. If this turns out to be the case, you should get out of the house and do something completely different.

## 19 SUNDAY
*Moon Age Day 23    Moon Sign Sagittarius*

The Moon arrives in your zodiac sign just in time for Sunday. You will be bright, happy and extremely reactive today. With everything to play for, plus a good dollop of luck working in your favour, it might be worth taking the odd small but measured chance and facing up to a few challenges today.

## 20 MONDAY
*Moon Age Day 24    Moon Sign Sagittarius*

This should be another generally good day for the sign of the Archer, with your popularity going off the scale and plenty of people wanting to know you. Although things are not quite so good that everything you touch turns to gold, you should find that you can get on well and you make a good impression on just about anyone.

## 21 TUESDAY
*Moon Age Day 25    Moon Sign Sagittarius*

If there is one thing you can be relied upon for at the moment it is fairness and even-handedness. Because you are showing yourself to be so honest and open with others, they are likely to return the favour, leading to a clearing of the air all round. There may be celebrations somewhere within the family and you will certainly wish to join in.

## 22 WEDNESDAY
*Moon Age Day 26    Moon Sign Capricorn*

Stay alert for possibilities at the moment. Certainly at work you should find that things are looking up for you and you can take advantage of situations that others don't even notice to further your own personal ambitions. Your general reaction time should be good and you are likely to be on the receiving end of a few favours.

## 23 THURSDAY
*Moon Age Day 27    Moon Sign Capricorn*

You are turning up the volume of your personality even more and it would be difficult for anyone to miss your presence at the moment. Although you come from behind in some competitive situations, you can still make the winning post first. Nothing marks you out more now than your ability to turn adversity into success.

## 24 FRIDAY
*Moon Age Day 28    Moon Sign Aquarius*

It might seem that you have everything you need right now, except money. It's true that this is not the most advantageous period of the year financially, or even the month. All you must do is show some patience and keep plugging away steadily. Take heart, because it won't be long before your efforts begin to bear fruit.

## 25 SATURDAY
*Moon Age Day 0    Moon Sign Aquarius*

This should be a fairly busy day, with plenty of opportunity to make new contacts. Family members might decide the time and weather is right to curl up in the warm, but that won't appeal to you at all. Getting the airing you need might mean looking up someone with a similar attitude to your own.

## 26 SUNDAY
*Moon Age Day 1    Moon Sign Aquarius*

If you want some excitement today, you are more than capable of going out and looking for it. What won't happen is adventure coming and tapping you on the shoulder. Sagittarius is full of enterprise all the time. For most Archers this is an ideal period for selling someone a product or an idea.

## 27 MONDAY
*Moon Age Day 2    Moon Sign Pisces*

A newer and better phase is on the way when it comes to getting your own way in material matters of almost any sort. This doesn't mean you are suddenly going to come into pots of money, merely that you organise what you do have better. Your present chatty nature can gain you some admirers.

## 28 TUESDAY
*Moon Age Day 3    Moon Sign Pisces*

The more you communicate today, the better are the chances you will get what you want from life. Personal attachments look particularly secure and it is very likely you will find yourself at the top of the popularity stakes. Confiding in someone you don't know all that well would probably not be a good idea.

# March
## 2017

## Your Month at a Glance

$\oplus$ = Opportunities are around    $\ominus$ = Be on the defensive    ● = Life is pretty ordinary

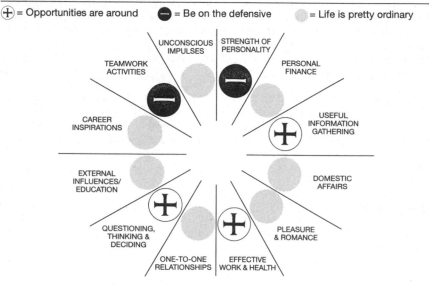

UNCONSCIOUS IMPULSES

STRENGTH OF PERSONALITY

TEAMWORK ACTIVITIES

PERSONAL FINANCE

CAREER INSPIRATIONS

USEFUL INFORMATION GATHERING

EXTERNAL INFLUENCES/ EDUCATION

DOMESTIC AFFAIRS

QUESTIONING, THINKING & DECIDING

PLEASURE & ROMANCE

ONE-TO-ONE RELATIONSHIPS

EFFECTIVE WORK & HEALTH

## March Highs and Lows

*Here I show you how the rhythms of the Moon will affect you this month. Like the tide, your energies and abilities will rise and fall with its pattern. When it is above the centre line, go for it, when it is below, you should be resting.*

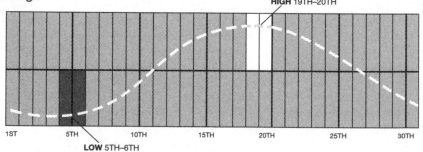

HIGH 19TH–20TH

1ST    5TH    10TH    15TH    20TH    25TH    30TH

LOW 5TH–6TH

## 1 WEDNESDAY
*Moon Age Day 4    Moon Sign Aries*

The middle of the week finds you anxious to take part in team activities, as well as perhaps needing to deal with mysteries of one sort or another. You are filled with curiosity at the moment, which could find its way to the surface in any one of a dozen different ways. In the workplace you should be operating with quick and accurate efficiency.

## 2 THURSDAY
*Moon Age Day 5    Moon Sign Aries*

There is a strong emphasis on communication today and it is very important to make sure that you are getting your message across as successfully as you can. Concentrate on doing one job at a time today, instead of the hundred you are sometimes inclined to take on. It is important to specialise and stick to what you are good at right now.

## 3 FRIDAY
*Moon Age Day 6    Moon Sign Taurus*

Harmonious domestic trends are present, allowing you to spend more time looking at the practicalities of life beyond your own front door. Those you care for, and especially your partner, are likely to be very attentive and make it plain that you are very important to them. The result is a greater sense of personal security.

## 4 SATURDAY
*Moon Age Day 7    Moon Sign Taurus*

If you find yourself to be impatient with practical matters, it is either because you are bored with them or simply that you need a change of scene. Do what you must today in order to feel more satisfied with life but beware of making any rash decisions when it comes to finances. It would be easy to lose money under present trends.

## 5 SUNDAY
*Moon Age Day 8    Moon Sign Gemini*

There are some things you simply cannot do entirely on your own, which is why you may be looking around for experts at the moment. Almost anyone will lend a hand if you are willing to ask for it. Socially and romantically, this ought to turn out to be a rather special sort of Sunday, despite the lunar low.

## 6 MONDAY
*Moon Age Day 9    Moon Sign Gemini*

You probably won't feel on top of the world today but on the other hand, you have no real desire to push yourself particularly hard either. Attitude is very important and your life is helped considerably if you try to remain optimistic. Keep in mind that the present lull will soon pass. Conforming to expectations could be the hardest job now.

## 7 TUESDAY
*Moon Age Day 10    Moon Sign Cancer*

Domestic issues now appear to be very rewarding. This is partly because you reserve most of your time for people at home and won't be quite so inclined to dash off at a moment's notice. People are especially fond of you and they should not be afraid to show it now, sometimes to the point of causing a little embarrassment.

## 8 WEDNESDAY
*Moon Age Day 11    Moon Sign Cancer*

Your personal charm can make a big impact on almost anyone right now and you will be less inclined to get on the wrong side of people than can sometimes be the case. Warm and sincere in your attitude, your desire to get involved in charitable pursuits is that much stronger and with you on board almost any enterprise is heading for success.

## 9 THURSDAY
*Moon Age Day 12    Moon Sign Leo*

Wonderful social events can be on the way but you may have to sort out a minor disaster at home or amongst friends before this can be the case. You adapt quickly and think well on your feet. These are the hallmarks of Sagittarius and they are certainly on display at the moment and for some days to come.

## 10 FRIDAY
*Moon Age Day 13    Moon Sign Leo*

An important discussion might fail to bring you exactly what you want, which will go down hard after a few days during which you have become used to getting your own way. Some compromise might be necessary but take comfort from the fact that it could actually lead to a greater measure of success than you were originally hoping for.

## 11 SATURDAY
*Moon Age Day 14    Moon Sign Virgo*

A charming and easy-going manner is something you have in abundance this Saturday and this can be turned to your advantage with no trouble whatsoever. If you get the chance to take those you care for by surprise go for it, and also be ready to make new social contacts at some stage during the day. Sagittarius is on a social roll this weekend.

## 12 SUNDAY
*Moon Age Day 15    Moon Sign Virgo*

Your sense of adventure is extremely strong and typical of your sign that means you will sometimes be taking risks. Of course if you didn't, you wouldn't be the sort of person you naturally are. There is a limit though, and you might need someone you care about to tell you when you are pushing your luck slightly too much.

## 13 MONDAY
*Moon Age Day 16    Moon Sign Virgo*

The area of love and romance is now favourably highlighted and you should find that the people you are fondest of are the ones who are showing you the greatest amount of attention. It won't always be possible to get your own way, even when you turn on the charm but you can cause a stir.

## 14 TUESDAY
*Moon Age Day 17    Moon Sign Libra*

Your mind is working overtime and it seems easy for you to assess how almost anyone is likely to behave under given circumstances. Not everyone appears to have your best interests at heart but they should come good when it matters the most. Don't be too quick to judge the actions of people you don't know well.

## 15 WEDNESDAY
*Moon Age Day 18    Moon Sign Libra*

Your mind is both quick and sharp, with a biting wit that can catch the people around you both at home and at work off guard. Most of what you say goes right to the mark but you might upset one or two people unintentionally. If you keep your level of sarcasm down to about half what it can be things should work out fine!

## 16 THURSDAY
*Moon Age Day 19    Moon Sign Scorpio*

Now you have even more energy and a greater sense of purpose in your physical activity, both at work and in social or sporting endeavours. Sagittarius at its best begins to show and you will be able to express yourself in the most positive way. This will gain you more popularity, which is often reward enough itself to the Archer.

## 17 FRIDAY
*Moon Age Day 20    Moon Sign Scorpio*

The odd and unusual in life once again becomes your main focus. Perhaps the deeper recesses of Sagittarius are showing? You are sometimes accused of being superficial but this isn't true at all. On the other hand, seeing the darkest recesses of your mind isn't too comfortable and you will probably decide to keep the lid in place anyway.

## 18 SATURDAY
*Moon Age Day 21    Moon Sign Scorpio*

The weekend brings some really good potential, particularly in terms of your home life. Life is centred on a fourth-house Sun and the way it supports the domestic qualities that surround you. There isn't much doubt that your family will be of even more importance at present than would usually be the case.

## 19 SUNDAY
*Moon Age Day 22    Moon Sign Sagittarius*

You now have absolutely no shortage of energy and the lunar high makes it possible for you to overcome obstacles that might have been around for quite some time. If you want to surprise yourself with your own versatility, now is the time to do so. Few can keep up with the pace you are likely to be setting at present.

## 20 MONDAY
*Moon Age Day 23    Moon Sign Sagittarius*

A word in the right ear can make a tremendous difference now and you should not hold back when it comes to testing the amount of influence you actually have. Push your luck all the way to its limit and use your intuition when it comes to discovering just how far you can go. Friends may be extra helpful and supportive during today.

## 21 TUESDAY
*Moon Age Day 24    Moon Sign Capricorn*

Any clouds that do appear today should have significant silver linings. It is important to look beyond any specific event and into the reason for it. Once you do this, you get a better understanding and can react more sensibly. There could be a quite a few compliments coming your way, most likely this evening.

## 22 WEDNESDAY
*Moon Age Day 25    Moon Sign Capricorn*

Today brings you face-to-face with the consequences of some of your past actions. This is by no means a bad thing because it is apparent you are putting problems right and behaving in a generally responsible way. Family-based projects will almost certainly figure largely in the midweek period but make some time for work if you need to as well.

## 23 THURSDAY
*Moon Age Day 26    Moon Sign Capricorn*

Unexpected visitors could slow down your routines and make life more difficult in some ways but you still feel the need to be as social as possible. This is a day of balance, when you can achieve a little of everything but perhaps not quite enough of anything. Maybe the best reaction is simply to smile. Jack-of-all-trades works on occasion!

## 24 FRIDAY
*Moon Age Day 27    Moon Sign Aquarius*

Romance shines out and draws you in at some stage today. This is especially true in the case of younger Archers or those who are specifically looking for love. Trends suggest that you should listen carefully to what is being said in your vicinity because even the most offhand comment can have far-reaching implications.

## 25 SATURDAY
*Moon Age Day 28    Moon Sign Aquarius*

A social weekend is very likely for Sagittarius. Romance continues to loom large in the minds of many Archers and you enjoy a high degree of popularity. Of course, you can't expect to be everyone's cup of tea but the people who don't care for you won't appeal too much in any case. There are many certainties in your head this weekend.

## 26 SUNDAY
*Moon Age Day 29    Moon Sign Pisces*

You need to feel as though you are in charge of your own destiny today, which might mean crossing swords with those who are trying to manipulate you in some way. Try to be diplomatic because you won't get anywhere if you are rude to anyone. Partnerships seem protected from negative trends.

## 27 MONDAY
*Moon Age Day 0    Moon Sign Pisces*

As the month wears on, so you get closer and closer to some of your most important objectives, particularly at work. Social trends are not quite so strong now and you could deliberately choose to spend more time on your own or in the company of the people you love and trust the most.

## 28 TUESDAY
*Moon Age Day 1    Moon Sign Aries*

You want to get things right if you can, but that might mean calling in the assistance of someone else. What you don't take kindly to at the moment is the assertion that you don't know what you are doing. Actually, it comes down to special skills in the end and we can't all be perfect at everything.

## 29 WEDNESDAY
*Moon Age Day 2    Moon Sign Aries*

There are many different forms of progress in the average life and you are looking for all of them at the same time today. Make the most of the fact that you should certainly find yourself more in charge in professional situations; whilst when it comes to co-operative ventures you clearly want to be in the driving seat.

## 30 THURSDAY
*Moon Age Day 3    Moon Sign Taurus*

There are a number of different sorts of people entering your life at this time. Some of them are going to be your type and others will not be. The type of person who fascinates you the most is the one who you don't instinctively like but who you nevertheless find interesting and even personally attractive. Try to look beyond superficiality to the real person.

## 31 FRIDAY

*Moon Age Day 4    Moon Sign Taurus*

You seem to be jumping around from foot to foot today. This is unusual because Sagittarius is almost never an indecisive zodiac sign. The mere fact that this happens can make you feel rather uncomfortable but all you really need are other matters to take control of your ever-active mind and you will find the focus you have been lacking.

# April

## Your Month at a Glance

⊕ = Opportunities are around    ⊖ = Be on the defensive    ● = Life is pretty ordinary

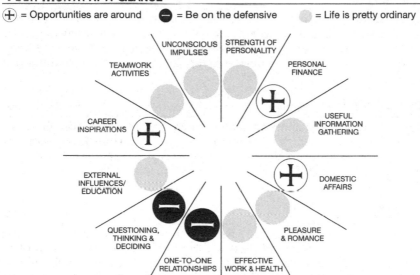

UNCONSCIOUS IMPULSES

STRENGTH OF PERSONALITY

TEAMWORK ACTIVITIES

PERSONAL FINANCE

CAREER INSPIRATIONS

USEFUL INFORMATION GATHERING

EXTERNAL INFLUENCES/ EDUCATION

DOMESTIC AFFAIRS

QUESTIONING, THINKING & DECIDING

PLEASURE & ROMANCE

ONE-TO-ONE RELATIONSHIPS

EFFECTIVE WORK & HEALTH

## April Highs and Lows

*Here I show you how the rhythms of the Moon will affect you this month. Like the tide, your energies and abilities will rise and fall with its pattern. When it is above the centre line, go for it, when it is below, you should be resting.*

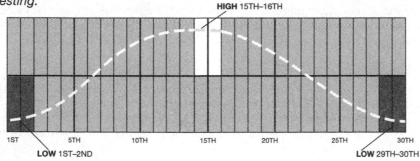

HIGH 15TH–16TH

1ST    5TH    10TH    15TH    20TH    25TH    30TH

LOW 1ST–2ND

LOW 29TH–30TH

## 1 SATURDAY
*Moon Age Day 5    Moon Sign Gemini*

Part of your mind goes forward, whilst another part of it travels into the past. Actually, that isn't such a bad thing because you have a good deal to learn at the moment from the way you have dealt with situations previously. Leave some time free to spend with someone who thinks you are the most wonderful person around.

## 2 SUNDAY
*Moon Age Day 6    Moon Sign Gemini*

You can expect a slightly slower day for Sunday. This will be particularly noticeable since things have been going so well during the last few days. The lunar low will prevent you from achieving quite the degree of understanding with others that has been possible of late but you can still enjoy yourself if you work at it.

## 3 MONDAY
*Moon Age Day 7    Moon Sign Cancer*

Taking chances in romantic situations could lead to a few complications and so really isn't worthwhile. It is true that you enjoy much popularity at present, which is generally the case, but there is always the danger that you can push things too far. In a practical sense, work hard today to give yourself a break later.

## 4 TUESDAY
*Moon Age Day 8    Moon Sign Cancer*

The overall emphasis that trends have placed on leisure recently remains in place today. As a result it is likely that for much of the next week you will be looking to have fun. Such is your state of mind that it is easy for you to find ways to amuse those around you – especially your partner and your best friends.

## 5 WEDNESDAY
*Moon Age Day 9    Moon Sign Leo*

A slight shift in emphasis brings you to an 'outdoor' frame of mind, which bearing in mind the advancing year is probably not so much of a surprise. You will also be quite intellectually motivated and anxious to travel to places that have a strong historical bias and which retain a heady atmosphere of the past.

## 6 THURSDAY
*Moon Age Day 10    Moon Sign Leo*

Though you might have to overcome an initial sense of lethargy regarding career and practical matters, things soon speed up and you find yourself making significant progress. The attitude of friends could puzzle you for a while, probably until you manage to get them talking and understand the root of the problem.

## 7 FRIDAY
*Moon Age Day 11    Moon Sign Leo*

There are plenty of good things coming your way, one or two of which you've waiting a long time to enjoy. You should be pretty much on top of the world and anxious to make the most of whatever life is offering. This is more than can be said for someone at home or maybe a very good friend.

## 8 SATURDAY
*Moon Age Day 12    Moon Sign Virgo*

Current personal and professional developments should continue to go generally your way. If you have any difficulty at all, it could be in the sphere of your family life. Younger family members especially are likely to play up and probably for no justifiable reason that you can see or understand. Take a few breaths and ride out the trend.

## 9 SUNDAY
*Moon Age Day 13    Moon Sign Virgo*

Curb your natural tendency to speak first and think later. Although most of Sunday is likely to be generally harmonious, there are one or two people around today who could irritate you slightly. Stop to realise that by speaking out you are only going to cause unnecessary atmospheres and difficult situations.

## 10 MONDAY  ☿
*Moon Age Day 14    Moon Sign Libra*

There are some dynamic influences around today and your mind is likely to be quick-fire and your reactions like lightning. Your life should be very busy this week and there could be every opportunity to take journeys, whether these turn out to be for the sake of business or for pleasure. Make the most of them in any case.

## 11 TUESDAY  ☿
*Moon Age Day 15    Moon Sign Libra*

Lots of planetary energy is now likely to be focused on your own needs and requirements. Like all Fire-signs, Sagittarius can have a slightly selfish streak from time to time, though now it appears that you help others as much as you do yourself. You should not find it hard to be confident in professional matters.

## 12 WEDNESDAY ☿
*Moon Age Day 16    Moon Sign Scorpio*

Your personal expectations are sometimes too high, particularly regarding your own capabilities. It may well be true that you can sometimes work near-miracles when you really go for it, but you know in your heart that this doesn't always work and in any case you don't always have the absolute support of other people. Be willing to settle for the very good today, instead of the amazing.

## 13 THURSDAY    ☿    *Moon Age Day 17    Moon Sign Scorpio*

When pressing ahead with long-terms plans, you need to make sure that everyone else concerned has been informed. There are people around who won't be very happy if they feel they have been bamboozled into something they don't want. It's really just a matter of sharing information and asking for opinions.

## 14 FRIDAY    ☿    *Moon Age Day 18    Moon Sign Scorpio*

You are unlikely to have quite as much influence over life as was the case yesterday. Twelfth house Moons always precede the lunar high and this month is no exception. The fact is that you are likely to be thinking about things a great deal and maybe taking time out from a hectic social life to do so.

## 15 SATURDAY    ☿    *Moon Age Day 19    Moon Sign Sagittarius*

**What a wonderful time this would be for putting new ideas and schemes into practice. You might think you are restricted from letting your hair down but you will manage to find a way somehow. Your confidence grows significantly, as much as anything because others are relying on you so willingly.**

## 16 SUNDAY    ☿    *Moon Age Day 20    Moon Sign Sagittarius*

**A large helping of good luck helps you towards your objectives at the moment and makes it possible for you to take the odd careful chance. Because your level of popularity is now so high, you willingly take part in all manner of social events and gatherings. This in turn increases your popularity and boosts your charisma.**

## 17 MONDAY    ☿    *Moon Age Day 21    Moon Sign Capricorn*

It is likely that your personal life will be more fulfilling than appears to have been the case for quite some time. Meanwhile, you may be deciding to address your physical wellbeing. If you have decided to embark on some new sort of regime, do make sure that you take it steadily at first.

## 18 TUESDAY    ☿    *Moon Age Day 22    Moon Sign Capricorn*

You can make some financial gains tomorrow, maybe off the back of the last couple of days. In the main though, you are likely to be more contemplative and quite happy to spend some time thinking things through. If someone in the family lets you down, there might be a sound reason for it so avoid an over-reaction.

## 19 WEDNESDAY ☿
*Moon Age Day 23    Moon Sign Capricorn*

Perhaps you prefer a diversity of interests at the moment? This would certainly seem to be what the present planetary line-up is indicating. However, there are certain issues that are presently difficult to avoid. Turning your attention towards them won't be too appealing but it could be necessary.

## 20 THURSDAY ☿
*Moon Age Day 24    Moon Sign Aquarius*

Intimate encounters with those you love today could put a different slant on issues that have been on your mind recently. Maybe you recognise that you have been taking things too seriously – or perhaps not seriously enough? Either way, there is food for thought and a slightly more thoughtful Archer comes to the fore.

## 21 FRIDAY ☿
*Moon Age Day 25    Moon Sign Aquarius*

Although you could lack a degree of patience with your partner or family members, you do need to exercise a little self-discipline today. The approach to the weekend can be good for all sorts of fun activities, especially if you are undertaking them alongside those who have the same desire to paint the town red as you presently do.

## 22 SATURDAY ☿
*Moon Age Day 26    Moon Sign Pisces*

This is definitely a good time to let go and be yourself. Don't be held back by negative types, something that would be far too easy today. Try to engage people in the sort of conversation that suits you best, keeping the subject matter varied and interesting. Most important of all, stay away from controversy.

## 23 SUNDAY ☿
*Moon Age Day 27    Moon Sign Pisces*

Your spirits are high and you could notice within yourself a kind of restlessness that can only be addressed by doing something stimulating and different. Whether everyone around you feels the same remains to be seen though you should find someone who is willing to go along for the ride with you.

## 24 MONDAY ☿
*Moon Age Day 28    Moon Sign Pisces*

Your chart suggests that there will be some tiresome aspects of life to deal with right now. Exactly what these may be is going to differ from Archer to Archer but for all of you your boredom threshold is low. The more you ring the changes, the less likely you are to demonstrate your inability to deal with tedious situations.

## 25 TUESDAY ☿ *Moon Age Day 0   Moon Sign Aries*

With the Sun now in your sixth house, you do have the power to change situations for the better. Not everyone shares your present view of the world or maintains the level of optimism that seems to come as second nature to you. Fortunately, convincing other people that you are right is also part of the Sagittarian package.

## 26 WEDNESDAY ☿ *Moon Age Day 1   Moon Sign Aries*

It would appear from prevailing planetary trends that almost the whole world is lining up to do you one favour or another. Do not turn away the help that is on offer, even when you are sure that you could do things better yourself. You need to be just as kind and tactful as proves to be possible today.

## 27 THURSDAY ☿ *Moon Age Day 2   Moon Sign Taurus*

There are emotional ups and downs to be dealt with today, though you are likely to be so busy in a practical sense that you may not even notice them. This could be disconcerting for your partner if he of she wishes to address specific issues. A good old-fashioned heart-to-heart talk is probably required so don't shy away from it.

## 28 FRIDAY ☿ *Moon Age Day 3   Moon Sign Taurus*

The things you learn at work today can have an important bearing on the future as a whole. It's definitely time to keep your eyes and ears open. Even the sort of gossip that you would normally avoid is worth your attention. In a personal sense, it is the small things of life that tend to make you happy now.

## 29 SATURDAY ☿ *Moon Age Day 4   Moon Sign Gemini*

Certain setbacks are more or less inevitable today, though if you know this is going to be the case, they won't throw you too much. A deeper sense of reasoning accompanies this month's lunar low, proving the adage that 'it's an ill wind that blows nobody any good'. Look out for personalities entering your life.

## 30 SUNDAY ☿ *Moon Age Day 5   Moon Sign Gemini*

Progress is still limited and at best you will take modest steps towards your objectives. Instead of throwing all your efforts into trying to make material gains, you might be better off thinking about your personal life, an area that will be more fortunate. Take some time to listen to the stories your loved ones are telling at present.

*May*

2017

## Your Month at a Glance

(+) = Opportunities are around     ● = Be on the defensive     ⬤ = Life is pretty ordinary

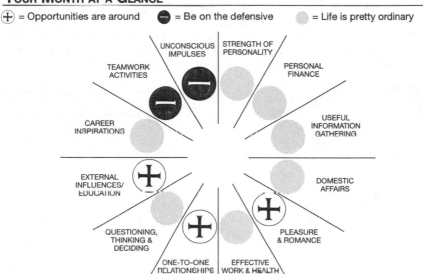

- UNCONSCIOUS IMPULSES
- STRENGTH OF PERSONALITY
- TEAMWORK ACTIVITIES
- PERSONAL FINANCE
- CAREER INSPIRATIONS
- USEFUL INFORMATION GATHERING
- EXTERNAL INFLUENCES/ EDUCATION
- DOMESTIC AFFAIRS
- QUESTIONING, THINKING & DECIDING
- PLEASURE & ROMANCE
- ONE-TO-ONE RELATIONSHIPS
- EFFECTIVE WORK & HEALTH

## May Highs and Lows

*Here I show you how the rhythms of the Moon will affect you this month. Like the tide, your energies and abilities will rise and fall with its pattern. When it is above the centre line, go for it, when it is below, you should be resting.*

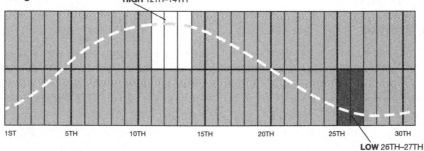

HIGH 12TH–14TH

1ST     5TH     10TH     15TH     20TH     25TH     30TH

LOW 26TH–27TH

## 1 MONDAY ☿ *Moon Age Day 6   Moon Sign Cancer*

Some useful information could be coming your way, probably from directions you least expected. You are more than ready to take decisions in isolation, if that's what it takes to get ahead. However, you are equally likely to be co-operative with others especially when they display a similar attitude.

## 2 TUESDAY ☿ *Moon Age Day 7   Moon Sign Cancer*

You have always had the advantage of a magnetic personality and an ability to create an impact but never more so than appears to be the case right now. Exciting romantic developments could come along at any time and may take you by surprise. You should be happy to join in with whatever is happening in your social group and may even suggest something.

## 3 WEDNESDAY ☿ *Moon Age Day 8   Moon Sign Leo*

Watch out for situations that are not at all as they appear. This would not be a good day for signing documents, unless you have had the time to look very carefully at the small print. Someone you haven't seen for a long time is likely to come along at any moment now and might bring a surprise or two with them.

## 4 THURSDAY *Moon Age Day 9   Moon Sign Leo*

There is a big emphasis on both your social and romantic life now. Keeping up with the rest of the world in a practical sense is a piece of cake and there will still be time to spare during which you show the warmest side of your nature. Charity work could be right up your street at any time now.

## 5 FRIDAY *Moon Age Day 10   Moon Sign Virgo*

Work and practical matters seem capable of running themselves at the moment. Meanwhile you see ways to have a good time and to lift the spirits of someone who is not very happy at present. Your confidence isn't in short supply but do make sure you know what you are talking about before you say too much.

## 6 SATURDAY *Moon Age Day 11   Moon Sign Virgo*

A change of scenery for the weekend would lighten your mood no end. You won't need too much encouragement in order to have a good time and you clearly know how to encourage other people to enjoy themselves too. Even normally solemn types should be willing to take off their socks and paddle now.

## 7 SUNDAY
*Moon Age Day 12    Moon Sign Libra*

With relationships now flourishing with a good deal more sparkle than they have had for a while you will be happy to take more notice of them. There are all sorts of people likely to come into your life around now and some of them hold a particular fascination for you. Don't be too willing to fall for a glib line or an attractive face, though.

## 8 MONDAY
*Moon Age Day 13    Moon Sign Libra*

Practical skills help you to get the best from life and it won't be hard now to mix business with pleasure in some way. Self-employed Archers might turn out to be the luckiest of all right now and there are no really difficult planetary influences standing around you today. Look for restful interludes when you can.

## 9 TUESDAY
*Moon Age Day 14    Moon Sign Libra*

Strong emotions underlie what you are saying and doing today, even if some people don't understand this. It would not be fair to criticise others for their treatment of you if they don't understand what they are doing wrong. To obviate the issue altogether, make sure you explain yourself fully.

## 10 WEDNESDAY
*Moon Age Day 15    Moon Sign Scorpio*

When it comes to getting your own way in personal relationships, you should have very little trouble at the moment. It is possible that Sagittarians who are between relationships at this time could see romance blossoming very soon. However, some might say you are presently too particular for your own good.

## 11 THURSDAY
*Moon Age Day 16    Moon Sign Scorpio*

Whilst your underlying ambition will tend to keep energy levels high, you are still likely to find yourself subject to an emotional and restless mood for much of the time. It's as though you can't quite decide what you want from life, or how to go about finding the path that is going to be right for you in the future. Don't worry unduly and wait for this trend to pass.

## 12 FRIDAY
*Moon Age Day 17    Moon Sign Sagittarius*

**You now enjoy a mental and physical peak, not to mention a time of significant popularity. With everything to play for it is almost certain you would be willing to take a few little chances, though this probably isn't necessary in order to get more or less what you want from life.**

## 13 SATURDAY
*Moon Age Day 18    Moon Sign Sagittarius*

Help comes from some unexpected places right now and it appears that some major ambitions are likely to be achieved either now or in the very near future. Getting your mind around problems that have taxed you in the past now seems to be a piece of cake. Be careful you don't ignore too many rules and regulations, as sometimes they are there for a reason.

## 14 SUNDAY
*Moon Age Day 19    Moon Sign Sagittarius*

Thanks to the lunar high your personal charisma is now very strong and it is unlikely that many could resist it. This may lead to you stealing the spotlight from others, something you occasionally do unintentionally. Yours can be a very dominant character but you are sensitive too, so make sure you don't deliberately upstage anyone.

## 15 MONDAY
*Moon Age Day 20    Moon Sign Capricorn*

Your ambitions at work could be really driving you forward now. If you are not employed or perhaps you are retired you will still be finding things to keep you occupied. You seem to be embarking on some sort of personal search but it would be sensible to itemise first what you are actually looking for.

## 16 TUESDAY
*Moon Age Day 21    Moon Sign Capricorn*

It might have failed to register to such a busy person as you that the summer has arrived. There is a wealth of planetary trends around you at present that indicate a definite need to run barefoot through the new-grown grass. If you can't manage that, at least get a breath of good fresh air this week.

## 17 WEDNESDAY
*Moon Age Day 22    Moon Sign Aquarius*

There may be exciting events happening today because of the lives of loved ones. This probably means you won't be the centre of attention, and as a Fire-sign that fact will not please you at all. An abiding lesson to be learned at present is that you can gain almost as much from the back of the queue as you can from the front.

## 18 THURSDAY
*Moon Age Day 23    Moon Sign Aquarius*

Along comes a period during which is quite possible for you to deal with several different tasks at the same time. Whether or not you achieve all your objectives in the way you would wish could be in doubt. What matters most is that you are happy with your lot and comfortable in your decisions.

## 19 FRIDAY                    *Moon Age Day 24    Moon Sign Pisces*

The emphasis today is on leisure and pleasure, in fact things have been moving in that direction since the start of the week. You won't want to concentrate on the mundane aspects of life any more than you are forced to and, given half a chance, you tend to skip gleefully from one social situation to another.

## 20 SATURDAY                    *Moon Age Day 25    Moon Sign Pisces*

Some tension is likely in emotional relationships this weekend, which is why it would be best to keep things light and airy. Deep and meaningful discussions are probably not a good idea because they could so easily turn into rows. In reality, you might prefer to mix with friends as much as possible and so avoid the situation altogether.

## 21 SUNDAY                    *Moon Age Day 26    Moon Sign Pisces*

Amongst those with whom you mix, you are the cream of the crop. Soaking up all this popularity isn't too difficult for Sagittarius but you must not allow it to go to your head. You are such a good self-publicist that, if you are not careful, you might end up believing your own spin, which lessons of the past should tell you is never a good thing.

## 22 MONDAY                    *Moon Age Day 27    Moon Sign Aries*

Getting into the good books of others isn't hard because it is so easy for you to turn on the charm. Confidence grows when you are dealing with situations you fully understand, though is less evident when you are out on a limb. Interruptions are probably inevitable today so just accept them, and enjoy the fact that some of them should be amusing.

## 23 TUESDAY                    *Moon Age Day 28    Moon Sign Aries*

The things that others do for you at this time can make you feel very lucky indeed, even though the favours that come your way are only small in scope. Maybe you are thinking more deeply but it's a fact that you recognise exactly where your bread is buttered and tend to respond positively to specific individuals.

## 24 WEDNESDAY                    *Moon Age Day 29    Moon Sign Taurus*

A rather fulfilling period in relationships comes along now. Co-operation, together with genuine give and take are the keywords that matter. Things are probably less clear-cut in working associations. Perhaps it is within professional matters that should take care not to come across as a little too pushy.

## 25 THURSDAY
*Moon Age Day 0    Moon Sign Taurus*

There are likely to be minor distractions around and these can definitely get in the way of progress in a practical sense. Some of these are entirely social in nature, so eradicating them is not going to be easy without avoiding friends altogether. In the end what you are looking for is compromise.

## 26 FRIDAY
*Moon Age Day 1    Moon Sign Gemini*

Keep life as simple as possible today and try to realise that you will get what you need right now, though probably not quite what you want. Happiness is so often a state of mind and you are philosophical enough at present to realise this. Participating in hobbies could appeal to you now.

## 27 SATURDAY
*Moon Age Day 2    Moon Sign Gemini*

Stay away from unnecessary arguments and show your kindest and most tolerant face to the whole world. You can easily disarm others by refusing to rise to their bait, leaving them looking foolish. The hero within you isn't far from the surface, as others should be willing to testify at this time.

## 28 SUNDAY
*Moon Age Day 3    Moon Sign Cancer*

Teamwork issues are now less satisfying than was probably the case in the middle of the month. Quite a few trends now show what an individualist you are likely to be. Stick close to people in whom you have natural confidence and don't be too quick to pass judgement on anyone's ideas for the moment.

## 29 MONDAY
*Moon Age Day 4    Moon Sign Cancer*

Look out for monetary increases. These may not be large, or come from directions you would particularly expect, but they should be useful. Some speculation is necessary if you really want to make financial progress, though you are not exactly in the best planetary position to go too far for now.

## 30 TUESDAY
*Moon Age Day 5    Moon Sign Leo*

Now is the time to exercise your mental powers and to show a few doubters exactly what you are capable of. Don't allow your enthusiasm to run away with you though. There are times for taking chances and there are also situations in which it would be foolish to gamble. Knowing the difference is what counts today.

## 31 WEDNESDAY
*Moon Age Day 6    Moon Sign Leo*

This is a good time focus on creative pursuits and also to give some attention to your home surroundings. The arrival of the summer might have put you in the mood to do some decorating or, if you can afford it, to supervise someone else doing it for you. Even some gardening isn't entirely out of the question now.

# June

2017

## YOUR MONTH AT A GLANCE

$\oplus$ = Opportunities are around  ⊖ = Be on the defensive  ● = Life is pretty ordinary

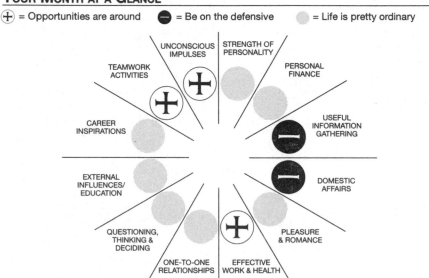

## JUNE HIGHS AND LOWS

*Here I show you how the rhythms of the Moon will affect you this month. Like the tide, your energies and abilities will rise and fall with its pattern. When it is above the centre line, go for it, when it is below, you should be resting.*

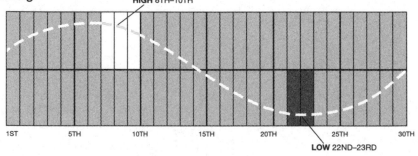

**HIGH** 8TH–10TH

1ST    5TH    10TH    15TH    20TH    25TH    30TH

**LOW** 22ND–23RD

## I THURSDAY
*Moon Age Day 7   Moon Sign Virgo*

Trends suggest that this should be a very productive period at work. Getting to grips with issues that have bugged you for some time won't be difficult. Look out for new friendships that will soon be coming your way, together with a change in the way you see long-term relationships. Some financial gains may also be possible.

## 2 FRIDAY
*Moon Age Day 8   Moon Sign Virgo*

It is quite likely that you will find yourself particularly good at solving problems right now, which is why you need to keep active today. Not only are you fun to have around, you know many of the answers that others are looking for. Keep up your efforts to persuade family members and friends to make more of themselves.

## 3 SATURDAY
*Moon Age Day 9   Moon Sign Virgo*

Whilst the Sun is in your solar seventh house you have the chance to understand those around you a little better than might have been the case in the past. You are more thoughtful and a good deal more diplomatic than you often are. Make the most of the improving sporting and general activity trends.

## 4 SUNDAY
*Moon Age Day 10   Moon Sign Libra*

You should be able to achieve a better understanding of those around you at this time and also come to terms with aspects of your own nature that you don't always address. People from the past can pay a return visit to your life around now and bring with them some interesting new possibilities and maybe a change of opinion for you.

## 5 MONDAY
*Moon Age Day 11   Moon Sign Libra*

There should be plenty of emotional support when you need it the most, together with a renewed sense of togetherness in the case of at least one relationship that might have looked rather tired of late. You are not short of confidence, or that extra oomph that might be necessary when you are at work.

## 6 THURSDAY
*Moon Age Day 12   Moon Sign Scorpio*

You are not about to miss a trick when it comes to handling problems of any sort. Even if you might sometimes run the risk of being accused of being slightly unethical, the fact is that you deal with matters in a way that is unique to you. As long as you achieve your objectives, which means others are happy too, that will be fine in your book.

## 7 WEDNESDAY
*Moon Age Day 13    Moon Sign Scorpio*

Business dealings and social relationships can look especially good under present trends but it becomes more and more obvious that change is necessary to your life at almost every level. Avoid confusion in relationships by explaining yourself as fully and as often as you are able to do.

## 8 THURSDAY
*Moon Age Day 14    Moon Sign Sagittarius*

**Lady Luck should now be on your side and all the power of your zodiac sign is present again. Although not everyone will be rooting for you, it probably won't be at all hard to bring others round to your own point of view. There are potential gains from a monetary point of view so keep your eyes open.**

## 9 FRIDAY
*Moon Age Day 15    Moon Sign Sagittarius*

**Press ahead with major ambitions and do whatever you can to make certain that others notice you are around. This shouldn't be at all hard under present trends and nor will be making a good impression at work. Your ideas are quite far-reaching and you have the verbal dexterity to put them across to others.**

## 10 SATURDAY
*Moon Age Day 16    Moon Sign Sagittarius*

**It is one-to-one relationships that seem to hold the most magical possibilities at this stage of the weekend, even though it could seem at first that you are going to be more or less fully committed to routines. There is much to be said for doing things in twos and everything to gain from sharing the best of what you are.**

## 11 SUNDAY
*Moon Age Day 17    Moon Sign Capricorn*

Good things can happen in both business and personal relationships, though the latter is more likely to be addressed on a Sunday. You remain active and happy to do whatever takes your fancy, which certainly means having fun. Confidence is the order of the day, as is that winning Sagittarian smile you are wearing.

## 12 MONDAY
*Moon Age Day 18    Moon Sign Capricorn*

Socially speaking it is possible that you will be more reluctant than usual to play any mind games today. You may feel the urge to spend time on your own, or at least in the company of people you see as being very close to you. Conventional thoughts pass you by and originality is virtually your middle name.

## 13 TUESDAY
*Moon Age Day 19    Moon Sign Aquarius*

The emotional aspects of life are very important to many Archers at the moment but you should not allow these to get in the way of the more outgoing side of your nature, which also has a strong role to play at present. People you care about deeply now have very special ways of showing their affection so listen to what they have to say.

## 14 WEDNESDAY
*Moon Age Day 20    Moon Sign Aquarius*

A strong urge for a more active social life is likely to overtake you in the middle of this week and this could mean that you are slightly less committed to your work than would normally be the case. This won't be too much of a problem because your sign is quite capable of combining work and leisure into one cohesive whole.

## 15 THURSDAY
*Moon Age Day 21    Moon Sign Aquarius*

You are now likely to be riding the crest of a social wave, which for the Archer is always preferable to quiet times. There are possible financial gains to be had and although these are not large they will be welcome all the same. Be certain before you embark on a new business venture, take solid advice and never be reckless where money is concerned.

## 16 FRIDAY
*Moon Age Day 22    Moon Sign Pisces*

Social matters and general encounters with others should prove to be both rewarding and interesting today. Be careful you don't offer inadvertent offence to colleagues, although it is within your nature to speak your mind and people usually take this at face value. Compromise is an important word today but so is integrity.

## 17 SATURDAY
*Moon Age Day 23    Moon Sign Pisces*

It is personal relationships that bring out the best in you today. Although you are still mixing freely with a number of different people, it is your partner or family members that figure the most. What an excellent time this would be to take a break, perhaps a well-earned day or two away?

## 18 SUNDAY
*Moon Age Day 24    Moon Sign Aries*

There is much of interest going on in the outside world and you won't be at the back of the queue when it comes to joining in. With plenty of energy, more than a smattering of good luck and an instinctive knowledge of how to behave, this can be a day to remember.

## 19 MONDAY
*Moon Age Day 25   Moon Sign Aries*

Casual contacts work best today and it is unlikely you will opt for intense romantic encounters or even meeting new people at present. In practical matters, you could be all fingers and thumbs, which is why you might even decide to leave most of them alone for the moment. Keep things light and bright for a day at least.

## 20 TUESDAY
*Moon Age Day 26   Moon Sign Taurus*

Make sure you are properly in the know regarding things that are expected of you today. You can't perform properly if you don't know what you are supposed to be doing. It might be time to ask one or two leading questions and if necessary to seek the help and advice of a professional or two.

## 21 WEDNESDAY
*Moon Age Day 27   Moon Sign Taurus*

Trends suggest that today can be very intense and also potentially frustrating for at least some Archers. The problem seems to be the present position of the Moon in your chart, which is inclined to lead to reappraisals of personal attachments, together with a flurry of new starts you didn't ask for or anticipate.

## 22 THURSDAY
*Moon Age Day 28   Moon Sign Gemini*

It might be the case that specific decisions are best left until another time. Your sense of responsibility is not especially high for the moment and you would much rather enjoy yourself than face too many serious issues. There's nothing at all wrong with having a short holiday and yours would do well to come now.

## 23 FRIDAY
*Moon Age Day 29   Moon Sign Gemini*

Entertainment brings out the best in you, whether you are creating it for others, or enjoying someone else's efforts. The Archer is generally fun to have around but rarely more so than at the moment. The fact that the lunar low is about is likely to get totally lost in the fun and frivolity today.

## 24 SATURDAY
*Moon Age Day 0   Moon Sign Cancer*

It would be a very good idea to vary your routines as much as you possibly can today. It appears that travel is positively highlighted, though managing to arrange it at short notice won't be too easy. Keep your ears open because this is a time when you might hear news that is definitely to your advantage.

## 25 SUNDAY
*Moon Age Day 1    Moon Sign Cancer*

If you keep your eyes open, you could get some material benefits before the day is out. This is potentially one of the best days of the month to make money, or at the very least to put yourself in a strong position for later on. By the evening, you are likely to have achieved much more than you may have expected.

## 26 MONDAY
*Moon Age Day 2    Moon Sign Leo*

In open debate you are especially good today but that doesn't mean you should deliberately go out and look for an argument. You need to be certain in your attitude but careful in the way you express yourself. It is possible for you to get much further with diplomacy than sheer word power.

## 27 TUESDAY
*Moon Age Day 3    Moon Sign Leo*

You might have to alter one or two of your plans today but your reaction time is good and there doesn't seem to be a great deal to hold you back. Friendship is of special importance at the moment and you need to make it plain to those close to you just how much they mean to you.

## 28 WEDNESDAY
*Moon Age Day 4    Moon Sign Leo*

Today it might not be easy to keep things on an even keel. Try to stay cool, even when you think there is some unnecessary provocation coming your way. You can sort out the consternation of a friend or a family member quite easily, so take the time to help them when you see your assistance is needed.

## 29 THURSDAY
*Moon Age Day 5    Moon Sign Virgo*

Things change quickly as the Moon moves on and in terms of relationships you should find yourself in good company today. There is no doubt that you are easy to get along with and that you are making more and more friends as a result. This is the Archer that everyone loves best. Make the most of these warm and happy trends.

## 30 FRIDAY
*Moon Age Day 6    Moon Sign Virgo*

A matter close to your heart occupies your attention now. Getting to grips with the mundane aspects of life won't be easy because you are looking to the wider horizons that represent the medium and long-term future. Be willing to join in with family celebrations, no matter who has organised them.

# July

2017

## Your Month at a Glance

⊕ = Opportunities are around   ⊖ = Be on the defensive   ⬤ = Life is pretty ordinary

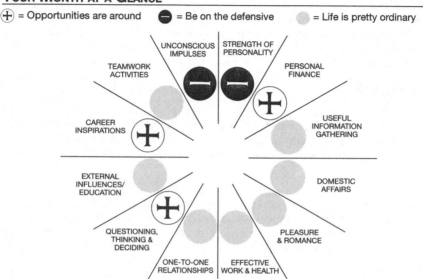

## July Highs and Lows

*Here I show you how the rhythms of the Moon will affect you this month. Like the tide, your energies and abilities will rise and fall with its pattern. When it is above the centre line, go for it, when it is below, you should be resting.*

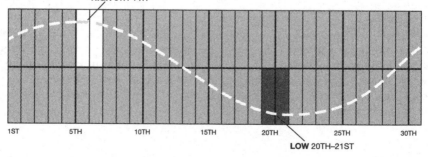

HIGH 6TH–7TH

LOW 20TH–21ST

1ST   5TH   10TH   15TH   20TH   25TH   30TH

## 1 SATURDAY
*Moon Age Day 7    Moon Sign Libra*

Any difficult changes you have had to implement of late could now be a thing of the past and you are better able to turn your mind wholeheartedly towards the future. With less clutter in your life, the way forward should look clearer. You have done all the spring-cleaning that is necessary for now.

## 2 SUNDAY
*Moon Age Day 8    Moon Sign Libra*

Today is likely to find you more than willing to make the most of the social possibilities that Sunday offers, happy to shine and eager to let others know you are around. Of course not everyone rates you, but it's impossible to be a Sagittarian and to get through life without one or two people showing a tad of jealousy or envy.

## 3 MONDAY
*Moon Age Day 9    Moon Sign Scorpio*

Whilst everyday matters warrant a more cautious approach and could be annoying, romance could well turn out to be the high spot as a new working week gets started. Progress generally continues but has as much to do today with what you are leaving behind, as what you can see in the future.

## 4 TUESDAY
*Moon Age Day 10    Moon Sign Scorpio*

Today you would be better off working as part of a team because in doing so you will draw strength from others and get on much better generally. There are certainly some gains to be made that involve you putting forward some fairly radical proposals and then watching for the reactions. The most important component for you now is flexibility.

## 5 WEDNESDAY
*Moon Age Day 11    Moon Sign Scorpio*

It may become clear that certain aspects of your daily life, or a relationship, are not running quite as smoothly as you would wish. Don't over-react to this state of affairs but show some patience. In another day the Moon will re-enter your zodiac sign but you will have to wait until then for life to be sparkling again.

## 6 THURSDAY
*Moon Age Day 12    Moon Sign Sagittarius*

**The tide turns and you find yourself in an excellent position to get ahead. The lunar high seems to back your most potent plans for the future and allows you to get a good hold on the way others are likely to react around you. Confidence grows and so does your ability to influence the world at large.**

## 7 FRIDAY *Moon Age Day 13   Moon Sign Sagittarius*

Everyday issues should now go according to plan and it appears that you may receive some unexpected help. Quick talk and speedy discussions pay the best dividends, if only because you recognise that to delay will cost profit at one level or another. Romantic matters also seem positively highlighted today.

## 8 SATURDAY *Moon Age Day 14   Moon Sign Capricorn*

Don't sit on the fence today. You will need to take a stance, even if this means making yourself slightly unpopular with someone. It won't be possible to agree with everyone and you will be much better off once you have committed yourself one way or another. Trust your own judgement in most matters, both business and personal.

## 9 SUNDAY *Moon Age Day 15   Moon Sign Capricorn*

Try to make this a very special day for yourself and your nearest and dearest. Although practical matters have a lot going for them, it is in the sphere of personal attachments and family values that you find the greatest happiness. This is a Sunday that was built for enjoyment and for showing your true feelings.

## 10 MONDAY *Moon Age Day 16   Moon Sign Capricorn*

A fulfilling period in terms of romance and pleasure seems to be the case as a new working week begins again. Anything old, unusual or curious is likely to captivate you now and you have a great fondness for intellectual pursuits. Look out for some strong support for your ideas coming from unexpected places.

## 11 TUESDAY *Moon Age Day 17   Moon Sign Aquarius*

Remember that there is only so much you can control on a practical level and you might need to rely on the advice, knowledge and skills of someone who is more in the know than you are. It's never easy to admit when you are out of your depth, but this could be necessary if you really want to get ahead in the next few days.

## 12 WEDNESDAY *Moon Age Day 18   Moon Sign Aquarius*

Emotional relationships still provide the most comfortable associations, while your professional life appears to be on hold just for the moment. The present planetary line-up shows that you might be about to spill the beans over an issue you have kept quiet about for ages – but do be careful who you tell.

## 13 THURSDAY
*Moon Age Day 19    Moon Sign Pisces*

It seems that there are forces at work that are helping you get more of what you want in a financial sense, though this isn't something you should push at the moment and you certainly must control your spending. Planning for the shorter-term is probably better than trying to look too far ahead for now at least.

## 14 FRIDAY
*Moon Age Day 20    Moon Sign Pisces*

Personal freedom is what seems to matter the most now, which is not at all unusual for the Archer. You need to do your own thing, which might go against the grain as far as certain other people are concerned. That can't be avoided because you will soon tire and start to fail if you feel fettered.

## 15 SATURDAY
*Moon Age Day 21    Moon Sign Aries*

Some hopeful information might be coming from far off places which could involve news of journeys you are likely to be making yourself before long. Keep an eye on your romantic partner and make certain that he or she understands how deep your caring goes. If you don't this might not be understood right now.

## 16 SUNDAY
*Moon Age Day 22    Moon Sign Aries*

A more acquisitive side of your nature begins to show itself, with the Moon entering your solar second house. Because it is the Moon that is involved, this is likely to be a short-term situation so don't allow it to gain control over you. You should also ask yourself if something you presently intend to buy is really necessary.

## 17 MONDAY
*Moon Age Day 23    Moon Sign Aries*

Some unfortunate trends today suggest a definite chance that a really good plan could fail to get off the drawing boards if you fail to organise yourself properly. Make sure to look well ahead and plan carefully. If you feel it is necessary to enlist the support of someone in the know don't fight shy of doing so.

## 18 TUESDAY
*Moon Age Day 24    Moon Sign Taurus*

You are impatient to see your ideas becoming realities but you can't rush any situation today. Take things slowly and steadily, making sure that you have dealt with every contingency. Creating the necessary mental space to dream some important dreams is another factor you should not dismiss today.

## 19 WEDNESDAY
*Moon Age Day 25    Moon Sign Taurus*

This is a very light-hearted period, during which you are pleased to meet new people. You are the typical Sagittarian at present and should be enjoying a degree of popularity. People from the dim and distant past could be making a return visit to your life before very long, and should bring some happy times with them.

## 20 THURSDAY
*Moon Age Day 26    Moon Sign Gemini*

Trends suggest that you may have to cope with some unexpected delays at the moment and with the Moon in your opposite zodiac sign there won't be very much you can do about them. On the plus side, people generally will seem to have your best interests at heart and should prove to be both courteous and helpful.

## 21 FRIDAY
*Moon Age Day 27    Moon Sign Gemini*

Make time for simpler pleasures at this stage of the week. If you try to push too hard in a practical sense you will no doubt come unstuck. The best of all worlds would be to spend more time today with family members and especially your partner. You need to be surrounded by those you trust.

## 22 SATURDAY
*Moon Age Day 28    Moon Sign Cancer*

Rewards come to you via the broadening of your general horizons and through travel. This would be an excellent time for Sagittarians to take a holiday, or merely to get away from the everyday grind for a few hours. Almost any sort of journey, long or short, would suit you, as long as it is undertaken for fun.

## 23 SUNDAY
*Moon Age Day 0    Moon Sign Cancer*

Various tests of your patience are apt to show up today. Since the Archer is not famed for his or her tolerance, you will have to work that much harder at the moment. There are possible gains coming from friendship, plus the hint of better times for some of you when it comes to love and relationships.

## 24 MONDAY
*Moon Age Day 1    Moon Sign Leo*

This is a period with plenty of opportunities for intimate get-togethers. If you had already decided that the time was right for a heart-to-heart talk with someone, now is the day for it. You are tolerant, kind and patient and you positively revel in situations that demand a great deal of assistance from you.

## 25 TUESDAY
*Moon Age Day 2    Moon Sign Leo*

If you have a bee in your bonnet regarding a specific matter, you should do something about it before the week gets any older. With an overdose of confidence, you are likely to take on all sorts of jobs that you would normally leave to experts. That's fine, but make sure that you check out all the details before you get cracking.

## 26 WEDNESDAY
*Moon Age Day 3    Moon Sign Virgo*

Current influences place great emphasis on the social side of your life. You could enjoy travelling far and wide at the moment, but this really depends if you can find the time to do so. The fact is that you are likely to be very busy in a host of different ways and there certainly won't be any opportunity to get bored.

## 27 THURSDAY
*Moon Age Day 4    Moon Sign Virgo*

Life is now altogether interesting across the board and made even better by the presence of people who are really important to you. There are moments today when you might doubt your own capabilities slightly though in the end you come up trumps. Listen to the advice of friends and heed any warning they offer you.

## 28 FRIDAY
*Moon Age Day 5    Moon Sign Libra*

Life is likely to remain stimulating and particularly eventful at the moment. There is just a slight tendency for you to feel that you are going round in circles regarding specific issues but you are more capable than you probably believe. Catching up with a few chores could prove to be more interesting than you had expected.

## 29 SATURDAY
*Moon Age Day 6    Moon Sign Libra*

Today's trends suggest that you will be interested and diverted by cultural matters and you won't be backward at coming forward when it comes to speaking your mind either. Put together a new package to deal with a family issue but don't be surprised if you feel more fatigued than you might have expected.

## 30 SUNDAY
*Moon Age Day 7    Moon Sign Libra*

Be as practical as you like today because it is that side of your nature that is working the best. Although you could find relatives difficult to deal with, in the main you remain certain of potential gains and anxious to please. What shows most of all today is that friendly Sagittarian nature.

# 31 MONDAY

*Moon Age Day 8    Moon Sign Scorpio*

The pursuit of outdoor interests should make the day go with a swing, particularly if you don't have to work. Although you are now quite competitive, this doesn't really extend to professional matters. With no real sense of ultimate responsibility at present you really want to have some fun.

# *August*

2017

## YOUR MONTH AT A GLANCE

⊕ = Opportunities are around    ⬤ = Be on the defensive    ⬤ = Life is pretty ordinary

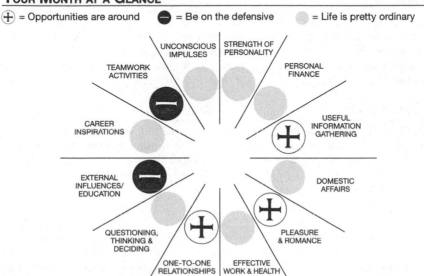

## AUGUST HIGHS AND LOWS

*Here I show you how the rhythms of the Moon will affect you this month. Like the tide, your energies and abilities will rise and fall with its pattern. When it is above the centre line, go for it, when it is below, you should be resting.*

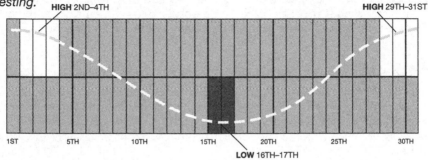

## 1 TUESDAY
*Moon Age Day 9    Moon Sign Scorpio*

Today it may be of paramount importance to show your partner how important they are. It doesn't take much to prove your love but this is worth a great deal in the longer-term. Although you are likely to be as busy as ever right now, take some time out to build a warm and romantic atmosphere. Money matters will be variable.

## 2 WEDNESDAY
*Moon Age Day 10    Moon Sign Sagittarius*

**Personal plans are on the up and you are now beginning what should turn out to be one of the most favourable periods during August. Your desire for change and diversity knows no bounds and this would be an excellent time for taking a holiday. Romance is also high on your personal agenda as the day wears on.**

## 3 THURSDAY
*Moon Age Day 11    Moon Sign Sagittarius*

**If you have some dreams that occupy your mind a great deal of the time, now is the time to make at least some of them into realities. Go for what you want with all guns blazing and believe in yourself. Even with the lunar high around you might not get to the sun but you could at least reach the moon.**

## 4 FRIDAY
*Moon Age Day 12    Moon Sign Sagittarius*

**Relationships established now with those you rely on at work are very important and it is clear that this period marks some sort of watershed in a professional sense. You can rethink old strategies and revolutionise the way you deal with certain specific matters. At home you might be called upon to lift the mood by being extra funny.**

## 5 SATURDAY
*Moon Age Day 13    Moon Sign Capricorn*

Friendship is a major force in your life now and it is possible that some new attachments will be made that are going to last a long time. Although you have many friends there are likely to be one or two whose presence in your life is especially important. You tend to make a real fuss of these special pals now.

## 6 SUNDAY
*Moon Age Day 14    Moon Sign Capricorn*

The desire for fresh fields and pastures new is extremely strong at the moment and makes you rather restless. You will still be able to get on with what is important in your day but you do need the fresh breeze of possibility blowing through your life. Don't restrict your horizons in any way and think big at all times.

## 7 MONDAY
*Moon Age Day 15    Moon Sign Aquarius*

You can now bring a work project to a satisfactory conclusion, maybe more in your mind than in reality. There might not be too much time for practical considerations today, especially if you have already made up your mind to spend a few hours with family members. The break will do you no end of good.

## 8 TUESDAY
*Moon Age Day 16    Moon Sign Aquarius*

Inspiration is fine but make sure you are not being carried away by illusions today. The thing is that you tend to see what you want to right now and may not be quite as realistic as would often be the case. People you don't see regularly may crop up now and can have a marked bearing on what happens in your life.

## 9 WEDNESDAY
*Moon Age Day 17    Moon Sign Pisces*

If you indulge your pleasures too much at the moment this could turn out to be an expensive time of the month. Much of what you would really enjoy now costs little or nothing and there is every reason to believe that the sort of friendship and support you value the most is with you throughout most of today and beyond.

## 10 THURSDAY
*Moon Age Day 18    Moon Sign Pisces*

This is a good time for throwing yourself into physical hard work. It's something that Sagittarius enjoys and the more you have to do, the greater is your level of energy. What would not suit you at all right now would be to find yourself sitting around and waiting. You need to make things happen if at all possible.

## 11 FRIDAY
*Moon Age Day 19    Moon Sign Pisces*

All home and family life matters, especially those that relate to the past in some way, are extremely important today. You need to actively spend more time with relatives, which might not be easy but is fairly crucial. It is possible to deal with a family issue that has been outstanding for quite some time now so grasp the nettle – you'll be glad you did.

## 12 SATURDAY
*Moon Age Day 20    Moon Sign Aries*

In a professional sense you now have a greater degree of power and influence and can make great inroads if you are at work. It doesn't matter what you do for a living, others are noticing how well you do it and you might be singled out for special treatment as a result. A career move isn't out of the question for some. Plan ahead for next week if you don't work on a Saturday.

## 13 SUNDAY ☿ *Moon Age Day 21 Moon Sign Aries*

This is a time during which you should feel the need to rid yourself of something you don't want and definitely don't need in your life. Perhaps this is a relationship that has run its course or even a job you are beginning to despise. This trend doesn't hit all Sagittarians with equal force but it should show itself in some way.

## 14 MONDAY ☿ *Moon Age Day 22 Moon Sign Taurus*

There are likely to be minor tensions about today, even though your intuition is strong and so you can probably see these coming. Don't get too serious about anything and others will follow your lead. Lightness of touch can defuse sensitive issues and prevent them from spoiling your day.

## 15 TUESDAY ☿ *Moon Age Day 23 Moon Sign Taurus*

Make sure you are on good terms with those at work, or if you are involved in education, your fellow students. It is from the direction of your co-workers that some of the best ideas are now likely to come. Be prepared to give away a little in terms of your own plans, in order to gain more through those of someone else.

## 16 WEDNESDAY ☿ *Moon Age Day 24 Moon Sign Gemini*

Don't leave work matters to chance at a time when your energy is at a low-ebb. You can begin to make necessary changes today but should apply yourself slowly and steadily. There are friends around at the moment who will do everything they can to prove their loyalty to you. Don't take this for granted, appreciate it.

## 17 THURSDAY ☿ *Moon Age Day 25 Moon Sign Gemini*

Your level of self-confidence is almost certain to be lower than you would wish and it will still be quite necessary to rely on the good offices of others if you want to get the very best from today. Don't be worried about a period of significantly less activity because this is both necessary and even useful when seen in its proper context.

## 18 FRIDAY ☿ *Moon Age Day 26 Moon Sign Cancer*

You need to feel fully in charge of situations today but the problem is that doing so isn't so easy. A few people at least seem to be getting in your way and proving to be especially difficult to deal with. Casual conversations can spark off some interesting ideas, particularly regarding work plans for later.

## 19 SATURDAY ☿     *Moon Age Day 27   Moon Sign Cancer*

In today's social encounters and discussions especially you tend to be reigning supreme. This is one of those periods in your life when it proves impossible to ignore just how popular you can be. It would be wise not to allow such considerations to go to your head because as in the old saying, 'pride goes before a fall'.

## 20 SUNDAY ☿     *Moon Age Day 28   Moon Sign Leo*

Extended negotiations and major decisions are likely to form part of the end of the weekend for you. The luckiest Sagittarians of all are those of you who are going on holiday today or tomorrow. For everyone else this would be an excellent time to start planning an eventful interlude.

## 21 MONDAY ☿     *Moon Age Day 29   Moon Sign Leo*

There is a great urge at present to put forward your point of view in an assertive manner. This is something you really should try to avoid. The fact is that you are going to be right most of the time and others will realise the fact. Driving the point home is more likely to alienate someone and is not necessary in any case.

## 22 TUESDAY ☿     *Moon Age Day 0   Moon Sign Virgo*

There is presently a strong emphasis on communication in your chart. There are quite a few planetary influences playing a part in this, not least of all Mercury. This is the sort of day that demands you speak out when you know you are right. This is especially true when you are supporting people who have less dynamism than you currently enjoy.

## 23 WEDNESDAY ☿     *Moon Age Day 1   Moon Sign Virgo*

There are some fortunate influences around now regarding career prospects. For those Archers who might presently be looking for a new job or between positions, you should concentrate your efforts at this time. Some of your personal objectives could be a little muddled at present but they should be sorted soon.

## 24 THURSDAY ☿     *Moon Age Day 2   Moon Sign Virgo*

Socially speaking you might be somewhat more reluctant than usual. There are a number of small astrological reasons for this state of affairs but none of them are so strong that they cannot be overcome. New contacts are on the cards, together with the chance of meeting pals from the past once again.

## 25 FRIDAY ☿ *Moon Age Day 3    Moon Sign Libra*

If you get the feeling that certain people are keeping you in the dark, it might be necessary to ask one or two leading questions. Your point of view in family matters is fair and valid, even if some people tend to suggest it is not. You need to walk the tightrope between getting your message across and going too far.

## 26 SATURDAY ☿ *Moon Age Day 4    Moon Sign Libra*

With a positive emphasis on personal security and finances a good deal of your time today could be taken up dealing with these matters. There are distractions at the moment and it is vitally important that you concentrate on what is really important to you. By the evening, you should be registering the fact that romantic prospects are good.

## 27 SUNDAY ☿ *Moon Age Day 5    Moon Sign Scorpio*

With plenty of support coming from your partner or family members, today should be quite happy and generally free from stress. Take the advantage of prevailing circumstances to have a rest, even if resting to you means climbing a mountain or going water skiing. Listen to the advice of a loved friend.

## 28 MONDAY ☿ *Moon Age Day 6    Moon Sign Scorpio*

It might be time for a step up the career ladder or perhaps you are willingly taking on extra responsibility in the hope that your efforts will be noticed later. Once again, you are working hard and putting in that extra bit of effort that can lead to great things. Don't be surprised if you are tired by the evening.

## 29 TUESDAY ☿ *Moon Age Day 7    Moon Sign Sagittarius*

**If you want to get the best from life, simply apply yourself and make the most effort you possibly can because this is what makes all the difference. Most trends are working for you and there are people around who seem to be just bursting to lend a hand. If there is any opposition to your point of view, now is the time to squash it.**

## 30 WEDNESDAY ☿ *Moon Age Day 8    Moon Sign Sagittarius*

**The planetary picture suddenly looks especially good for you. Not only are you supported by the position of the Sun but also you should be extra lucky whilst the lunar high is around. This really is the very best of times to concentrate your efforts and show the world what you are made of.**

## 31 THURSDAY ☿

*Moon Age Day 9    Moon Sign Sagittarius*

Try to make this a special day for yourself and everyone you come across. You can be the brightest, happiest and most rewarding person to know. The Archer is working at its best and true to your sign those comments you are making are like arrows and go straight to their intended mark.

# September

2017

## Your Month at a Glance

⊕ = Opportunities are around ⬤ = Be on the defensive ⬤ = Life is pretty ordinary

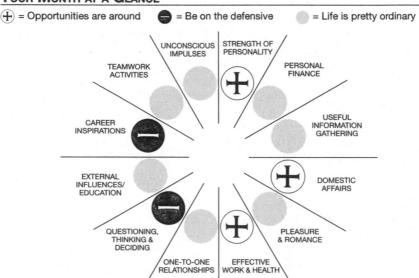

## September Highs and Lows

*Here I show you how the rhythms of the Moon will affect you this month. Like the tide, your energies and abilities will rise and fall with its pattern. When it is above the centre line, go for it, when it is below, you should be resting.*

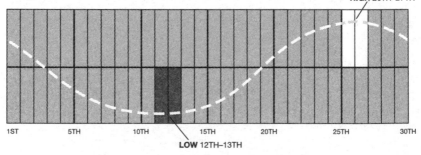

**HIGH** 26TH–27TH

1ST  5TH  10TH  15TH  20TH  25TH  30TH

**LOW** 12TH–13TH

## 1 FRIDAY ☿ *Moon Age Day 10 Moon Sign Capricorn*

You may find yourself to be rather involved in all sorts of activities at the moment. In particular you could discover that younger people begin to figure more prominently in your life but since you are always young at heart yourself that won't matter. Romantic opportunities are also possible, even if you weren't looking for them.

## 2 SATURDAY ☿ *Moon Age Day 11 Moon Sign Capricorn*

It is time to get a move on when it comes to making decisions that are going to have a bearing on your life for some time to come. Don't leave decisions to chance though. Think things through carefully and if you know it is necessary, seek out the advice of someone whose integrity and experience you trust.

## 3 SUNDAY ☿ *Moon Age Day 12 Moon Sign Aquarius*

There is a strong social theme running through your life at present and you tend to get on well with lots of different sorts of people. Even casual conversations can have far-reaching implications and you should not dismiss anything you hear at the moment without at least giving it due consideration.

## 4 MONDAY ☿ *Moon Age Day 13 Moon Sign Aquarius*

There could be a tendency to overlook small but essential details today. It is very important to concentrate on the matter in hand, even though there may be many thoughts and ideas clouding your mind. Keep abreast of news and current events because later in the day this sort of knowledge will prove essential.

## 5 TUESDAY ☿ *Moon Age Day 14 Moon Sign Aquarius*

Along comes a fairly important period of self-determination, which will continue for quite some time. Get financial details sorted out today and be willing to do whatever it takes to get the details of your life into shape. Conforming to the expectations of those around you may not be easy and you might not even be inclined to try.

## 6 WEDNESDAY ☿ *Moon Age Day 15 Moon Sign Pisces*

A day of striving for positive ambitions comes along now. The present position of the Sun favours decisive actions on your part. Other planetary alignments take care of popularity and put you very much in the winning seat for the days that lie ahead. Take moments out for specific projects that appeal to you.

## 7 THURSDAY ☿ *Moon Age Day 16   Moon Sign Pisces*

What would really suit you down to the ground is a total change. Even if the weather is not perfect, you would gain from being out of doors and from doing something that really pleases you. Stay in the company of those you really like and enjoy all the laughs that can come your way on a better-than-average and very social day.

## 8 FRIDAY ☿ *Moon Age Day 17   Moon Sign Aries*

Prepare for a good deal of lively interaction and enjoy the cut and thrust of a fairly typical Sagittarian sort of day. Your social life should be quite eventful and there is enough going on to keep you happy, though not so much that you find it difficult to focus on important matters. Perhaps a busy day at work then a Friday night out is on the cards.

## 9 SATURDAY ☿ *Moon Age Day 18   Moon Sign Aries*

This is a day on which to mobilise your reserves of strength and determination. There are gains to be made but you may have to work that bit harder in order to fully realise your potential. This won't stop you from enjoying yourself too and there isn't any doubt about the Archer's social inclinations at this time.

## 10 SUNDAY ☿ *Moon Age Day 19   Moon Sign Taurus*

This would be a good time to simply reflect and to understand your situation in life as it stands right now. Work out how you feel about yourself and what you want to do in order to be more secure. Happiness is quite genuinely a state of mind to Sagittarius much of the time and you may well realise the fact at present.

## 11 MONDAY ☿ *Moon Age Day 20   Moon Sign Taurus*

Relationships and the way they are presently working could spark off some interesting ideas that you will want to look at closely around now. Listen to your intuition today because it is finely tuned and unlikely to let you down. There is more genuine enjoyment to be had than has been the case for perhaps a week or so.

## 12 TUESDAY ☿ *Moon Age Day 21   Moon Sign Gemini*

The monthly lull patch begins. That's fine if you are relaxing on a beach somewhere because you will barely notice it. If, on the other hand, you are expected to work at full pitch for the whole day, you could find yourself to be somewhat tired by the evening. Try to pace yourself and rest when you can.

## 13 WEDNESDAY
*Moon Age Day 22     Moon Sign Gemini*

A brief rest probably isn't too much to ask for after what has been an eventful and in some way tiring couple of weeks. Not even the Archer can keep going at full speed all the time. There are plenty of people around who will be happy to take the strain and who can even give you some new incentives for later.

## 14 THURSDAY
*Moon Age Day 23     Moon Sign Cancer*

Friendships and partnerships are central to your success around this time. No matter whether an association is a personal or a professional one, it is when you are pooling your resources with someone else that you arrive at the very best conclusions. Competition doesn't worry you – in fact you find it stimulating.

## 15 FRIDAY
*Moon Age Day 24     Moon Sign Cancer*

Progress in a career sense may now depend on your ability to think on your feet. That shouldn't be much of a problem for most Archers but you could be up against some fairly determined characters. When it matters the most you are able to make the sort of friends who prove to be very supportive.

## 16 SATURDAY
*Moon Age Day 25     Moon Sign Cancer*

This could prove to be an extremely useful day when it comes to problem solving. With great enthusiasm and a little more planetary help some progress is more than likely. An ideal time for romance, with young or young-at-heart Archers leading the field. All sporting activities are well highlighted.

## 17 SUNDAY
*Moon Age Day 26     Moon Sign Leo*

Social highlights count for a great deal now, leading to what could be a fairly exciting and particularly interesting sort of Sunday. Don't allow yourself to get stuck in any sort of rut but push onward towards your destination. This advice applies to most of September and it certainly holds good at the moment.

## 18 MONDAY
*Moon Age Day 27     Moon Sign Leo*

The more independent your approach to life is at present, the greater are likely to be the rewards. Don't be left at the back of the queue at work but push your way forward and insist that your voice is heard. All the same, although controlling your own destiny seems all-important you can afford to give some ground without losing out in the end.

## 19 TUESDAY
*Moon Age Day 28   Moon Sign Virgo*

Some of you will consider this to be quite a nothing sort of day but if this is the case you probably are not watching closely enough. It's the things that happen beneath the surface that count the most. When it comes to dealing with people you don't know very well, intuition could be your best guide.

## 20 WEDNESDAY
*Moon Age Day 0   Moon Sign Virgo*

The things that happen today, socially or in a cultural sense, could prove to be very important in the weeks to come. This is no time to take your eye off any ball. Although you are generally perceptive right now, there is just a slight chance that you could be somewhat fooled later in the day.

## 21 THURSDAY
*Moon Age Day 1   Moon Sign Libra*

The things you encounter on a personal level today make for a generally interesting time. Don't expect to get too far ahead in a material sense and settle for a good second place, rather than passing the winning post through any sort of foul. Your behaviour towards others and the way it is seen is so important.

## 22 FRIDAY
*Moon Age Day 2   Moon Sign Libra*

There are some opportunities for monetary gains at this time, mainly thanks to the position of the Moon. Romantic attachments are well-starred and you could even discover an admirer or two you weren't aware of. Family discussions may lead you to thoughts of changes you would like to make in and around your home.

## 23 SATURDAY
*Moon Age Day 3   Moon Sign Scorpio*

Even the most casual conversations can prove to be both interesting and rewarding around now. Don't close your ears to any sort of gossip because even this brings clues as to how you should behave in the days ahead. Trends also suggest that your curiosity may be stimulated by some distinctly odd behaviour from others.

## 24 SUNDAY
*Moon Age Day 4   Moon Sign Scorpio*

The impact of your cheerful personality remains generally strong, so it isn't hard to get what you want from life, or to exert a positive influence on people along the way. Romance is a possibility, perhaps coming from an unexpected direction. Alternatively, an old flame could be rekindled this Sunday.

## 25 MONDAY
*Moon Age Day 5    Moon Sign Scorpio*

You feel the need to go off in search of new intellectual experiences as this working week gets underway. If your career is not supplying you with the sort of stimulus you require it might be necessary to find it elsewhere. Those people who can't keep up with your lightning-quick thought processes are likely to be left behind.

## 26 TUESDAY
*Moon Age Day 6    Moon Sign Sagittarius*

**Push ahead as quickly as you can with important dreams and schemes. The lunar high makes achieving at least some of these a real possibility and you should be as optimistic as can be around now. Although you won't get everything you are looking for at the moment, you are certainly likely to benefit from the overall auspicious trends.**

## 27 WEDNESDAY
*Moon Age Day 7    Moon Sign Sagittarius*

**What an excellent time this would be to put your persuasive powers to the test. There probably are not many people who would fail to be swayed by your silver tongue and your winning ways. Your confidence remains essentially high, even when you are being persuaded to do something you are not really sure about.**

## 28 THURSDAY
*Moon Age Day 8    Moon Sign Capricorn*

Although things are getting better and better from a social point of view they don't maintain the same sort of momentum in material matters or professional situations. Keep it light and simple, that's the recipe for success this Thursday. Since you are quite lucky under present trends, what about a shopping expedition?

## 29 FRIDAY
*Moon Age Day 9    Moon Sign Capricorn*

Some confusion is indicated, particularly regarding arrangements of any sort. Check and double-check details and, if necessary, make some follow-up telephone calls. You are certainly not in an argumentative frame of mind at this time though some of the people you have to deal with could be.

## 30 SATURDAY
*Moon Age Day 10    Moon Sign Capricorn*

This would be a good time to seek a breath of fresh air. Many Sagittarians will have made the decision early in the year to take a late holiday around now. If you are one of them your choice was a wise one. You need time to recharge flagging batteries, whilst at the same time thinking up new ideas.

# October
2017

## YOUR MONTH AT A GLANCE

⊕ = Opportunities are around     ⊖ = Be on the defensive     ⬤ = Life is pretty ordinary

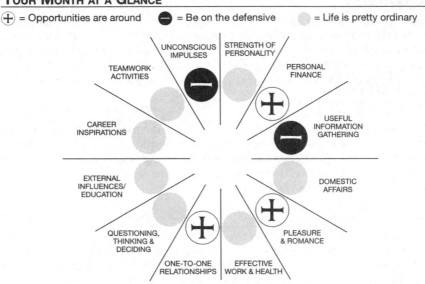

UNCONSCIOUS IMPULSES
STRENGTH OF PERSONALITY
TEAMWORK ACTIVITIES
PERSONAL FINANCE
CAREER INSPIRATIONS
USEFUL INFORMATION GATHERING
EXTERNAL INFLUENCES/ EDUCATION
DOMESTIC AFFAIRS
QUESTIONING, THINKING & DECIDING
PLEASURE & ROMANCE
ONE-TO-ONE RELATIONSHIPS
EFFECTIVE WORK & HEALTH

## OCTOBER HIGHS AND LOWS

*Here I show you how the rhythms of the Moon will affect you this month. Like the tide, your energies and abilities will rise and fall with its pattern. When it is above the centre line, go for it, when it is below, you should be resting.*

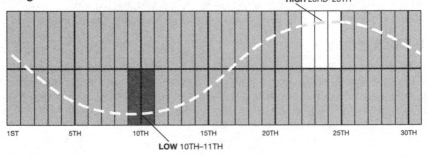

HIGH 23RD–25TH

1ST     5TH     10TH     15TH     20TH     25TH     30TH

LOW 10TH–11TH

## 1 SUNDAY
*Moon Age Day 11    Moon Sign Aquarius*

The focus is now on friendships and especially on those attachments that have been important to you for a long time. It is possible that you might be able to show great support to a pal today and to return a favour. As far as family members are concerned, one or two of them might be difficult to predict at present.

## 2 MONDAY
*Moon Age Day 12    Moon Sign Aquarius*

There may be conflict at work and it will be important to take the heat out of situations if at all possible. Although not everyone appears to be your friend at the moment it is difficult to understand why this should be the case. Just be yourself and awkward types should come round in the end.

## 3 TUESDAY
*Moon Age Day 13    Moon Sign Pisces*

This is a time for imagination and for looking at situations in unusual ways. Certainly your intuition is likely to be good and your ability to understand what makes other people tick has probably never been better. Casual conversations can lead to a new and quite unique way of dealing with people and family members especially.

## 4 WEDNESDAY
*Moon Age Day 14    Moon Sign Pisces*

Your need to get ahead in life could clash with the opinions and desires of other people around you. This won't be an issue as long as you are willing to listen to alternative points of view. Of course this has to be more than simply just paying lip service, you will need to really take note and perhaps revise your plans accordingly.

## 5 THURSDAY
*Moon Age Day 15    Moon Sign Aries*

The intensity of your views, particularly at work, gets you noticed but is it for the right reasons? There are times when you can be a little too outspoken for your own good and it is quite important to allow others to have their say. The failure to do so is something of a negative trend during this part of October.

## 6 FRIDAY
*Moon Age Day 16    Moon Sign Aries*

Stay confident and life will go your way. Although you cannot expect absolutely everyone to be on your side at present, when it matters the most people should come good for you. You can expect this to be a very pleasant period and one during which you can make gains as a result of your past efforts.

## 7 SATURDAY
*Moon Age Day 17    Moon Sign Taurus*

You can get a lot done now as a result of sheer self-discipline, not a quality that the Archer universally understands. Once you have made up your mind to a specific course of action you are unlikely to change it. Routines are now easily dealt with and some of them might be actively welcomed.

## 8 SUNDAY
*Moon Age Day 18    Moon Sign Taurus*

Meetings with very interesting people may set this Sunday apart for you. If you are taking a well-earned holiday from the practical aspects of life make sure that you don't load yourself up with a lot of different responsibilities instead. Today you need to drop the reins and behave like a ten-year-old just for a few hours.

## 9 MONDAY
*Moon Age Day 19    Moon Sign Taurus*

There is quite a strong chance that the beginning of this week will coincide with the feeling that your life in general is in a state of fluctuation. On a positive note, you are better able to deal with such a situation than most zodiac signs would be and you won't worry unduly if you are forced to think on your feet a good deal.

## 10 TUESDAY
*Moon Age Day 20    Moon Sign Gemini*

The arrival of the lunar low might not even be noticed and there are a couple of reasons why this could be the case. There are some very supportive planetary influences around right now and in any case you are not seeking to get on too quickly or pushing very hard. Stay relaxed and beat the position of the Moon.

## 11 WEDNESDAY
*Moon Age Day 21    Moon Sign Gemini*

Various circumstances should be working in your favour today. This should be a smooth running period and one during which your natural charm really pays off. Very few people could refuse your seemingly modest requests at the moment and you should have plenty of new friends.

## 12 THURSDAY
*Moon Age Day 22    Moon Sign Cancer*

This is a day during which some organisation and self-discipline could work wonders. It might occur to you that certain elements of your life have been running rather out of control and you will want to do something about this situation as soon as you can. That's fine but don't go at things like a bull at a gate.

## 13 FRIDAY
*Moon Age Day 23   Moon Sign Cancer*

You might want to ignore responsibilities almost totally today, in favour of socializing. There should be little to stop you seeking a good time and there are plenty of people around who will be only too willing to follow your lead. Planetary trends help on the romantic front and love could come knocking on your door at some point today.

## 14 SATURDAY
*Moon Age Day 24   Moon Sign Leo*

You should be putting your ingenuity to good use today and won't be stuck for a good idea at any stage. Avoid unnecessary routines because these will prove tedious and without any real merit. What you are looking for now is diversity and the chance to manage old jobs in your revolutionary new way.

## 15 SUNDAY
*Moon Age Day 25   Moon Sign Leo*

Although some of the things that go through your mind right now are only in the planning stage, you have a tremendous ability to make some of them workable. Don't ignore the little voice at the back of your mind that tells you when the time is right to act. There is little that remains beyond your grasp under present planetary influences.

## 16 MONDAY
*Moon Age Day 26   Moon Sign Virgo*

You might find it inspiring to seek out new contacts today, as well as getting a great deal from people who figure in your life more prominently than they have done in the past. Personal relationships should be looking good and you also have more than a slight chance of getting ahead of the game in the financial stakes. A good day all round!

## 17 TUESDAY
*Moon Age Day 27   Moon Sign Virgo*

It should be easier to achieve what you want today, particularly since you are in a good position to pick up on the support of colleagues, a few of whom think you are the bee's knees at present. A few unforced errors are possible but such is the force of your personality that you should manage to get yourself out of them without a struggle.

## 18 WEDNESDAY
*Moon Age Day 28   Moon Sign Libra*

You are still getting to where you want to go, even if the going is somewhat tough. Finding yourself up against it isn't necessarily a bad thing because it brings drive, zeal and enthusiasm. Sagittarius is not a zodiac sign that particularly respects or wants a smooth ride and often works best when it doesn't get one.

## 19 THURSDAY
*Moon Age Day 29    Moon Sign Libra*

Social and teamwork matters are favourably highlighted now, leading to a feeling that you can get on well with anyone in the world. Perhaps you are slightly more considerate regarding the feelings of those around you. Trends also suggest that Sagittarius is in a creative mood around now, so perhaps this will lead to a decorating spree at home?

## 20 FRIDAY
*Moon Age Day 0    Moon Sign Libra*

Although this won't be the most eventful day of the month, it does offer potential when it comes to thinking things through. With an absence of specific events in the diary and not too much excitement to deal with, you have an uncluttered perspective. That's got to be a first, so use it wisely.

## 21 SATURDAY
*Moon Age Day 1    Moon Sign Scorpio*

The friendly assistance that comes from the direction of people you know, as well as strangers, is bound to be especially well received today. This ought to be a bright and breezy sort of day, without too much in the way of perceived responsibility but with plenty of entertainment and fun.

## 22 SUNDAY
*Moon Age Day 2    Moon Sign Scorpio*

If this isn't exactly a Sunday to remember in a material sense, it can be quite good romantically. Others are noticing your presence, and if you are single maybe even people you have had liked for a while and wanted to get to know better. If the feelings are reciprocated, you could be in for a memorable sort of evening.

## 23 MONDAY
*Moon Age Day 3    Moon Sign Sagittarius*

**The lunar high can open up a multitude of new possibilities this time round and it will certainly speed things up a little. For those of you who have been feeling somewhat left behind, there are now new incentives and better monetary prospects. Doing more than one job at a time is quite easy now.**

## 24 TUESDAY
*Moon Age Day 4    Moon Sign Sagittarius*

**This would be a lucky day for making decisions of just about any sort. But life is not all about having to make your mind up. On the contrary, you have time on your hands and plenty of incentive to do something simply because it would be good fun. Your verbal dexterity is likely to come in very handy now.**

## 25 WEDNESDAY                    *Moon Age Day 5    Moon Sign Sagittarius*

You are now in the market for a good time. Sexy and keen to make a good impression Sagittarius puts on its best display at the moment. Don't be surprised if your flirtatious ways lead to encounters you might not have expected, though. It looks possible that not everyone you attract is your intended target.

## 26 THURSDAY                    *Moon Age Day 6    Moon Sign Capricorn*

Whilst concentration on detailed work could suffer today, in a general sense you are up for fun. It won't be easy to do everything you would wish, though you don't feel over committed to much right now. Sagittarius loves to have fun and this week is looking like it will provide that commodity in abundance.

## 27 FRIDAY                    *Moon Age Day 7    Moon Sign Capricorn*

Your main focus today is likely to be on your domestic life. Not much ruffles your feathers at the moment, though you won't take too kindly to being told what to do. This only really applies if you are at work today. Most home-based situations ought to be relaxing and comfortable.

## 28 SATURDAY                    *Moon Age Day 8    Moon Sign Aquarius*

If you work on a Saturday, professional matters should go smoothly today, even if inside yourself you would rather be somewhere else. It isn't the things you want to do that matter right now but rather the things you have to do. As long as you keep a smile on your face, the day should prove to be a breeze.

## 29 SUNDAY                    *Moon Age Day 9    Moon Sign Aquarius*

A slight lack of confidence or commitment typifies what happens to the Archer under today's planetary trends. Don't despair. This time is given to you in order that you can get your head together for the very real efforts you will be putting in soon. Accept it as a much-needed rest from your usually hectic pace.

## 30 MONDAY                    *Moon Age Day 10    Moon Sign Pisces*

It is close partnerships of any kind that make life most fulfilling now, both in a romantic sense and for those of you who are in co-operative professional ventures. Keep a sense of proportion regarding family matters, some of which appear to be giving you a slightly hard time right now. If you remain calm, the disharmony will pass soon.

## 31 TUESDAY

*Moon Age Day 11    Moon Sign Pisces*

Having moved steadily towards some of your life's goals in the recent past, your chart today suggests that you will now find yourself at some sort of cross-roads. That means looking again at issues and deciding where your effort is best concentrated henceforth. A chat with your partner or other family members could help.

# *November*
### 2017

---

## YOUR MONTH AT A GLANCE

(+) = Opportunities are around    ⊖ = Be on the defensive    ● = Life is pretty ordinary

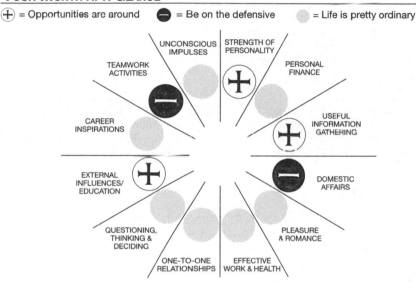

- UNCONSCIOUS IMPULSES
- STRENGTH OF PERSONALITY
- TEAMWORK ACTIVITIES
- PERSONAL FINANCE
- CAREER INSPIRATIONS
- USEFUL INFORMATION GATHERING
- EXTERNAL INFLUENCES/ EDUCATION
- DOMESTIC AFFAIRS
- QUESTIONING, THINKING & DECIDING
- PLEASURE & ROMANCE
- ONE-TO-ONE RELATIONSHIPS
- EFFECTIVE WORK & HEALTH

---

## NOVEMBER HIGHS AND LOWS

*Here I show you how the rhythms of the Moon will affect you this month. Like the tide, your energies and abilities will rise and fall with its pattern. When it is above the centre line, go for it, when it is below, you should be resting.*

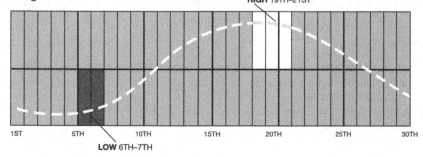

**HIGH** 19TH–21ST

**LOW** 6TH–7TH

1ST   5TH   10TH   15TH   20TH   25TH   30TH

## 1 WEDNESDAY
*Moon Age Day 12   Moon Sign Pisces*

You make your way in life by creating new ideas and coming up with different sorts of concepts and nothing is different about that situation now. Sagittarius is extremely innovative at the moment and others would be sensible if they took notice of what you have to say. Friends should be especially attentive today.

## 2 THURSDAY
*Moon Age Day 13   Moon Sign Aries*

You enjoy travel at the best of times but will take to it extremely well at present. There is something extremely attractive about simply getting on a train or in the car and setting off. It doesn't matter whether you are travelling for business or fun, it's the getting there that appeals you during today.

## 3 FRIDAY
*Moon Age Day 14   Moon Sign Aries*

A charming social performance on your part could impress any number of people. Astrological trends point to a rather unusual sort of day and a time during which you could easily be surprised. Not everyone might behave exactly as you had expected and you will need some flexibility to cope with this situation.

## 4 SATURDAY
*Moon Age Day 15   Moon Sign Taurus*

Emotional issues could prove to be somewhat demanding at the moment and you might decide to shelve them for a while. It would be best to keep yourself busy in other ways. Certainly there is no shortage of things to be done, either at work or at home, and it is possible that you will be quite busy on the social front.

## 5 SUNDAY
*Moon Age Day 16   Moon Sign Taurus*

All aspects of communications are going extremely well now. With some entertaining people on the horizon and almost everything going your way, the time has come to put your thoughts into tangible form. Almost anyone will be pleased to hear what you have to say and their reactions could be surprising.

## 6 MONDAY
*Moon Age Day 17   Moon Sign Gemini*

A mixture of some confusion and not a little incompetence could be the order of the day unless you take extra care. The Moon isn't doing you any favours and you really do need to call on the help and support of others in order to get the very best out of today. All in all, it might be best to stay tucked up in bed if you can.

## 7 TUESDAY
*Moon Age Day 18    Moon Sign Gemini*

You still won't be moving any mountains but you can enjoy yourself in quiet ways and maybe get to know someone close to you better than has been the case for quite a while. The more active and enterprising side of your nature is there, at least where making plans are concerned, though the activity has to come later.

## 8 WEDNESDAY
*Moon Age Day 19    Moon Sign Cancer*

You will probably go to great lengths to please others today. There's nothing wrong with this, except for the fact that you are likely to be disappointed with the response you get. Nevertheless the self-sacrificing quality you presently show isn't something you can alter. It's simply the way you are at this time.

## 9 THURSDAY
*Moon Age Day 20    Moon Sign Cancer*

Your energy levels are now plentiful and you will have little or no difficulty in getting what you need from life, even if you cannot manage everything you want. Routines are something you would not welcome around now and it is quite obvious that you are up for as much variety as you can get. Ring the changes if you can.

## 10 FRIDAY
*Moon Age Day 21    Moon Sign Leo*

Communications work in your favour now so keep the lines open in order to get more of what you want the most. There is also a slightly inward-looking tendency developing and this means that it isn't so much a matter of what you achieve that counts so much as why. Confidence remains the key and the world marvels at your versatility and ability to roll with the punches.

## 11 SATURDAY
*Moon Age Day 22    Moon Sign Leo*

A little false optimism could end up causing you some problems today, so it is worthwhile checking details at every stage and making certain the figures add up in terms of finances. You might not be feeling particularly cash-rich at the start of this weekend but you do retain a great deal of important influence – and you know deep down that money isn't everything.

## 12 SUNDAY
*Moon Age Day 23    Moon Sign Virgo*

A social or leisure activity might take something of a toll on you, which is why you could be slowing things down somewhat today. This seesaw time is nothing particularly unusual for Sagittarius and you cope with it almost without thinking. Respond to the warmth being shown to you by others.

## 13 MONDAY

*Moon Age Day 24   Moon Sign Virgo*

You should feel at harmony with the world as a whole and won't have too much difficulty coming to terms with others, even people who have gained a reputation for being rather awkward. Someone you mix with on a regular basis might be enjoying a little of the star status around now and it's likely to rub off.

## 14 TUESDAY

*Moon Age Day 25   Moon Sign Libra*

It looks as though life will now be as busy than ever, with material considerations taking the centre stage. It would be sensible to get practical matters out of the way early in the day, allowing time for relaxation and for mixing with people whose company you find particularly exciting.

## 15 WEDNESDAY

*Moon Age Day 26   Moon Sign Libra*

Get ready to go out and explore the wide blue yonder. Sagittarius is restless now and that certainly means the need for change. There are those around who might be trying to clip your wings in some way but you will find the means to get what you want in any case. You are quite determined to get what you want at present.

## 16 THURSDAY

*Moon Age Day 27   Moon Sign Libra*

Today is likely to be harmonious in almost every sense. Good contacts with useful people could set the day apart and might find you gaining financially from discussions or transactions. Your enjoyment of life knows no bounds, though you tend to express it in a somewhat low-key fashion whilst the Sun occupies your twelfth house.

## 17 FRIDAY

*Moon Age Day 28   Moon Sign Scorpio*

Today you might not be thinking clearly and may require the added help and support of people who are more in the know than you are. Eating humble pie, in order to get the information you need, is never a pleasurable experience for the Archer but you can content yourself with the knowledge that it is good for your soul.

## 18 SATURDAY

*Moon Age Day 0   Moon Sign Scorpio*

It is easy to tell today how many people hold you in high esteem. You could be surprised at the number, particularly since you learn you are popular with a few people you didn't think liked you at all. Don't be slow when it comes to asking for what you want, especially in a material sense.

## 19 SUNDAY
*Moon Age Day 1     Moon Sign Sagittarius*

The Moon races into your zodiac sign, bringing to an end the somewhat sticky period that has prevailed over the last three weeks or so. All is brightness and optimism for Sagittarius now and if you don't realise this, you are not looking hard enough. Treat awkward situations to a dose of good old-fashioned common sense.

## 20 MONDAY
*Moon Age Day 2     Moon Sign Sagittarius*

This should prove to be an industrious period, though there might not be much time for enjoyment. Sagittarius is on full alert now and making the most of every opportunity that comes along. How important is that though, if you don't manage to have some fun along the way? Try to strike a balance at all times now.

## 21 TUESDAY
*Moon Age Day 3     Moon Sign Sagittarius*

Things go well when you work in a team and you are at your best when co-operation with others is needed today. Although you can be a little offhand with people you don't like, in the main you are charm itself. At work it is possible that rules and regulations you deem to be unnecessary will irritate you. If so, try to rise above it.

## 22 WEDNESDAY
*Moon Age Day 4     Moon Sign Capricorn*

Keep your eye on the news today, whether newspaper or internet, because there could be things happening in your local area that are of special interest to you. It's time to make the most of any and every opportunity that comes your way and you won't want to be left out in the cold if there is any chance to get ahead of the pack.

## 23 THURSDAY
*Moon Age Day 5     Moon Sign Capricorn*

Make more time to look into the deeper side of life today. Spiritual concerns could be on your mind or at the very least you will want to feed your inner self. Along with this your intuition is likely to be working well and it won't take you long to suss out almost anyone with whom you come into contact.

## 24 FRIDAY
*Moon Age Day 6     Moon Sign Aquarius*

There is plenty to keep you occupied mentally but it might be worthwhile staying active in a physical sense too. This could be the ideal time to be thinking about getting fit, or at the very least enjoying some new kind of activity. Find a way to tone up those muscles, whilst at the same time enjoying yourself.

## 25 SATURDAY
Moon Age Day 7   Moon Sign Aquarius

You have plenty of personal power now and can have a great bearing on the sort of things that are happening around you. Don't let anyone tell you that you are not influential. The only way to satisfy yourself in anything today is to have a go and to thumb your nose at the opposition.

## 26 SUNDAY
Moon Age Day 8   Moon Sign Aquarius

There isn't a great deal of logic about today and it appears that at least part of the time you are running on automatic pilot. Although you might find certain people difficult to deal with, you do have great persuasive powers at present and merely have to remind yourself to use them properly.

## 27 MONDAY
Moon Age Day 9   Moon Sign Pisces

The Sun in your solar first house is really beginning to show its influence now. After a slightly sluggish period, you are now right back on form and already starting the run-up to Christmas. This is a time when the Archer wants to have fun and you shouldn't have too much trouble finding people who are willing to join in.

## 28 TUESDAY
Moon Age Day 10   Moon Sign Pisces

New avenues of communication tend to open up during this, the most potentially interesting of times. Although it might sometimes be further to the winning post that you might have imagined, it is worth keeping on running in almost any situation. The end of November can be truly yours with only a modicum of effort.

## 29 WEDNESDAY
Moon Age Day 11   Moon Sign Aries

Professional objectives do need to be handled especially carefully right now. There are possible small defeats in view, and you won't take at all kindly to these. Think before you act and if you are in any doubt, don't act at all. You will have the chance now to be involved in social gatherings that require little from you except your presence.

## 30 THURSDAY
Moon Age Day 12   Moon Sign Aries

If communications have been up in the air recently, you should find them easier today. You are regaining your full voice, though this is not a day to chance your luck too much. Your confidence in situations you know and understand well is high and these are the areas of life on which to concentrate.

# December
2017

## YOUR MONTH AT A GLANCE

⊕ = Opportunities are around  ⊖ = Be on the defensive  ⊙ = Life is pretty ordinary

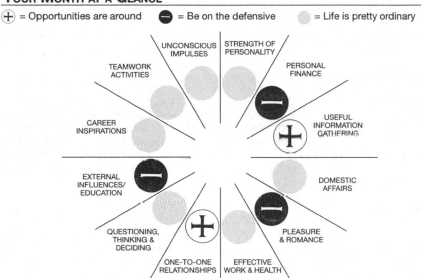

UNCONSCIOUS IMPULSES
STRENGTH OF PERSONALITY
TEAMWORK ACTIVITIES
PERSONAL FINANCE
CAREER INSPIRATIONS
USEFUL INFORMATION GATHERING
EXTERNAL INFLUENCES/ EDUCATION
DOMESTIC AFFAIRS
QUESTIONING, THINKING & DECIDING
PLEASURE & ROMANCE
ONE-TO-ONE RELATIONSHIPS
EFFECTIVE WORK & HEALTH

## DECEMBER HIGHS AND LOWS

*Here I show you how the rhythms of the Moon will affect you this month. Like the tide, your energies and abilities will rise and fall with its pattern. When it is above the centre line, go for it, when it is below, you should be resting.*

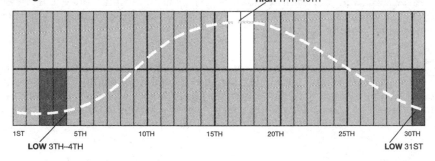

**HIGH** 17TH–18TH

1ST   5TH   10TH   15TH   20TH   25TH   30TH

**LOW** 3TH–4TH

**LOW** 31ST

## 1 FRIDAY
*Moon Age Day 13   Moon Sign Taurus*

An easy-going attitude descends today and might be assisted by some very good news coming in for a relative or friend. In your estimation, someone is having a run of good luck you consider to be well overdue. The less selfish qualities of the Archer are on display, which makes you good to be around and adds even more to your popularity.

## 2 SATURDAY
*Moon Age Day 14   Moon Sign Taurus*

A kind of power struggle seems to be about to take place now. If you are not a weekend worker, this trend is likely to have a bearing on your home life. Although it might seem attractive to be at the head of everything, you must accept that even at home there are some situations you simply don't understand and which you should leave alone.

## 3 SUNDAY ☿
*Moon Age Day 15   Moon Sign Gemini*

The monthly lull comes into operation, although this is somewhat mitigated by the present position of the Sun, which is especially helpful to you between now and Christmas. All the same, this might be a better time for planning than for putting your schemes into action. Be wary of bargains that look too good to be true. They probably are.

## 4 MONDAY ☿
*Moon Age Day 16   Moon Sign Gemini*

If you want a day during which you can make an impact on the world, this is not it. Instead of trying to do everything yourself, allow others to take at least part of the strain. This does not mean you are likely to lose control, so don't get upset about a fairly compulsory layoff that only lasts a day. Pace yourself and take things steadily, and trends will gradually improve.

## 5 TUESDAY ☿
*Moon Age Day 17   Moon Sign Cancer*

Personal objectives should be kept within easy reach today or you could find that you are stretching yourself more than is really necessary, unnecessarily so as it should now be a little easier to get what you want from life. Almost everyone loves you at the moment, even people who haven't shown you that much regard in the past.

## 6 WEDNESDAY ☿
*Moon Age Day 18   Moon Sign Cancer*

You look to home and family for the sort of support that might be missing out there in the wider world. With a slightly greater tendency to withdraw into yourself it will be clear to those who know you well that you have things on your mind. Don't allow petty concerns to turn into full-scale worries.

## 7 THURSDAY ☿ *Moon Age Day 19  Moon Sign Leo*

The finer things of life prove to be extremely important to you on this December Thursday. It isn't just that you are that fond of luxurious things, but more that you feel that to have them proves your success and status. Since such issues are currently at the forefront of the Sagittarian mind, there is no wonder they feature heavily today.

## 8 FRIDAY ☿ *Moon Age Day 20  Moon Sign Leo*

This is the time when you can really benefit from the help and support of loved ones. Christmas is not far away and the chances are that this is more or less the first time that the fact has really struck home. Gather all your family members together and delegate a few jobs that see that things get underway.

## 9 SATURDAY ☿ *Moon Age Day 21  Moon Sign Virgo*

Every one of us learns something new with each passing day. This is clearly true in your case, and particularly so with regard to the way you view personal attachments. Concentrating on the job at hand isn't going to be too easy but this won't matter because you need to focus on more cerebral matters.

## 10 SUNDAY ☿ *Moon Age Day 22  Moon Sign Virgo*

Nostalgia tends to be on the agenda this Sunday but of course this is a double-edged sword. It can thwart some of your intents but there are still important lessons to be learned. Get together with good friends if you can right now, maybe to do some shopping or enjoy a relaxed outing to somewhere new.

## 11 MONDAY ☿ *Moon Age Day 23  Moon Sign Virgo*

It's time to spread your wings somewhat and a new week offers some particularly interesting challenges. It is even possible that you will find just the thought of Christmas getting in the way of the sort of progress you really want to be making at this time and some slight frustration could be the result.

## 12 THURSDAY ☿ *Moon Age Day 24  Moon Sign Libra*

A plan of action that is meant to be played out on the professional stage may slow down or even come to a halt. This is something you are going to have to accept because you can't really alter the situation for the moment. Concentrate instead on your personal life and on home-based matters.

## 13 WEDNESDAY ☿
*Moon Age Day 25    Moon Sign Libra*

It might seem difficult to retain control over certain issues and it will probably be necessary to enlist some help. Admitting you are out of your depth isn't easy for a Sagittarius but it can save a lot of problems further down the road. The attitude of people you care about can be puzzling but in a more humorous than worrying way.

## 14 THURSDAY ☿
*Moon Age Day 26    Moon Sign Scorpio*

It could be that for some Archers there will be some small difficulties surrounding an intimate relationship. Getting this sorted out will be your number one priority. Meanwhile you are also busy in a practical sense but still more than willing to share some of your professional and expert knowledge with others.

## 15 FRIDAY ☿
*Moon Age Day 27    Moon Sign Scorpio*

Trends suggest a great deal of coming and going today, so much so that you might find it difficult to actually concentrate on anything at all. Maybe that's no bad thing. Specifics are not what your life is about right now and working with approximations and a little guess-work is part of the Archers key to success in any case.

## 16 SATURDAY ☿
*Moon Age Day 28    Moon Sign Scorpio*

A period of high-energy period begins today. At least some of it is likely to be dedicated to thoughts about Christmas, with arrangements being made all the time now. The social aspect of the holiday is more likely to appeal to you than the tinsel and trappings. Where family members are concerned, you might simply have to pretend to like that side!

## 17 SUNDAY ☿
*Moon Age Day 29    Moon Sign Sagittarius*

Along comes the influence that can supercharge the present period as far as you are concerned. The lunar high makes it possible for you to get more of what you want, as always, and also to help others to enjoy themselves too. Such is the positive impact of your personality right now that very little is out of your reach – even things that previously seemed impossible.

## 18 MONDAY ☿
*Moon Age Day 0    Moon Sign Sagittarius*

The ability to get your own way with others certainly looks like a notable talent of yours today and this is emphasised by the continuing position of the Moon. Good luck should attend you in every area, and might lead you to a small amount of speculation. If there is a job you want to do today you can polish it off in no time at all.

## 19 TUESDAY   ☿
*Moon Age Day 1   Moon Sign Capricorn*

A day of much moving about is forecast, though that won't prevent you from looking deeply into specific matters that are of personal interest to you right now. With communication very much to the fore, you should find telephone messages and emails flying in all directions for most of the day. Take time to absorb them carefully and think about what they have to say.

## 20 WEDNESDAY ☿
*Moon Age Day 2   Moon Sign Capricorn*

One-to-one relationships are the area of life that brings the greatest potential pleasure at this time. Don't work too hard, even though you might be trying hard to get as much done as you can before the holidays. What isn't addressed properly now will almost certainly wait. It's time to relax.

## 21 THURSDAY   ☿
*Moon Age Day 3   Moon Sign Capricorn*

There is a certain irrepressible quality about you today that almost everyone is going to notice. If you were sensible, you won't have pushed yourself too hard yesterday. Now, with energy to spare, you are really starting with enthusiasm on the road that leads to a very merry Christmas.

## 22 FRIDAY   ☿
*Moon Age Day 4   Moon Sign Aquarius*

An influence comes along that boosts moneymaking, though this close to Christmas it could be as much as a result of good luck as of good management. You have plenty to look forward to in a social sense but, as ever, you won't be able to please all the people all the time. Really bowling over one or two might be a good place to start.

## 23 SATURDAY
*Moon Age Day 5   Moon Sign Aquarius*

Try to set aside some time today to express your inner feelings. In the hustle and bustle of life these sometimes get overlooked. It doesn't take very long to say 'I love you', and these three little words can mean so much to the person you say them to. In a material sense you could find things coming your way that you didn't expect at all.

## 24 SUNDAY
*Moon Age Day 6   Moon Sign Pisces*

New love could be coming along for some Archers, particularly those who have been searching for new beginnings. Your confidence is generally high at the moment though you will have your work cut out keeping as many balls in the air as you are juggling right now. Don't forget, Christmas is only a day away.

## 25 MONDAY
*Moon Age Day 7    Moon Sign Pisces*

With a wealth of social invitations and a great deal of diversity on offer, Sagittarius should be really on the ball for Christmas Day. As you begin to realise the scope of what is on offer, it becomes more difficult to be everywhere at the same time. It certainly shouldn't be hard to have a good time.

## 26 TUESDAY
*Moon Age Day 8    Moon Sign Pisces*

You will enjoy being on the go now and should be responding positively to all the exciting invitations that come your way. There is no way that you can do everything that others would wish, though you are quite prepared to try. If you have time to get out to the sales, you could be on your way to a genuine bargain.

## 27 WEDNESDAY
*Moon Age Day 9    Moon Sign Aries*

This is a really good day for gathering new information, as well as for interpreting the facts and figures of life in a new and innovative way. Still enjoying a little of the Christmas spirit, you won't be unduly stressed at present, although one or two family members could be. Try to offer the help you can and provide a listening ear.

## 28 THURSDAY
*Moon Age Day 10    Moon Sign Aries*

It is the interesting information offered to you today that keeps you both entertained and happy. The Archer is now very definitely a party animal and you are clearly making up for any quiet periods that attended Christmas itself. The message of the season isn't lost on you when it comes to people who are less well off than you are.

## 29 FRIDAY
*Moon Age Day 11    Moon Sign Taurus*

You can expect a good response today, not only from your partner and people you know, but also from strangers. You share well and will be happy to offer specific people the benefit of your experience. But it works both ways and if you keep your eyes and ears open, there is much to learn from others at present.

## 30 SATURDAY
*Moon Age Day 12    Moon Sign Taurus*

Avoid trivia. It's time to concentrate, even though in some senses that is the last thing you want to do right now. Although you are not short of common sense, you may feel as if there are people around who have it as one of their main objectives to confuse you. It's up to you to spot them and to take the right action.

# 31 SUNDAY                    *Moon Age Day 13    Moon Sign Gemini*

Life in all its variety is on offer to you at this time and this should lead to a few really good ideas that are going to be of great use to you in the new year. You are almost certain to be partying tonight and stand a chance of making a good impression but beware of the lunar low which might make you tired.

# How to Calculate Your Rising Sign

Most astrologers agree that, next to the Sun Sign, the most important influence on any person is the Rising Sign at the time of their birth. The Rising Sign represents the astrological sign that was rising over the eastern horizon when each and every one of us came into the world. It is sometimes also called the Ascendant.

Let us suppose, for example, that you were born with the Sun in the zodiac sign of Libra. This would bestow certain characteristics on you that are likely to be shared by all other Librans. However, a Libran with Aries Rising would show a very different attitude towards life, and of course relationships, than a Libran with Pisces Rising.

For these reasons, this book shows how your zodiac Rising Sign has a bearing on all the possible positions of the Sun at birth. Simply look through the Aries table opposite.

As long as you know your approximate time of birth the graph will show you how to discover your Rising Sign.

Look across the top of the graph of your zodiac sign to find your date of birth, and down the side for your birth time (I have used Greenwich Mean Time). Where they cross is your Rising Sign. Don't forget to subtract an hour (or two) if appropriate for Summer Time.

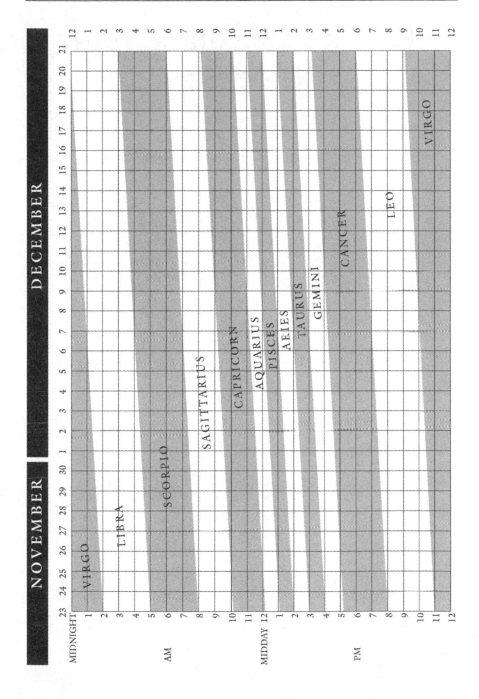

# THE ZODIAC, PLANETS AND CORRESPONDENCES

The Earth revolves around the Sun once every calendar year, so when viewed from Earth the Sun appears in a different part of the sky as the year progresses. In astrology, these parts of the sky are divided into the signs of the zodiac and this means that the signs are organised in a circle. The circle begins with Aries and ends with Pisces.

Taking the zodiac sign as a starting point, astrologers then work with all the positions of planets, stars and many other factors to calculate horoscopes and birth charts and tell us what the stars have in store for us.

The table below shows the planets and Elements for each of the signs of the zodiac. Each sign belongs to one of the four Elements: Fire, Air, Earth or Water. Fire signs are creative and enthusiastic; Air signs are mentally active and thoughtful; Earth signs are constructive and practical; Water signs are emotional and have strong feelings.

It also shows the metals and gemstones associated with, or corresponding with, each sign. The correspondence is made when a metal or stone possesses properties that are held in common with a particular sign of the zodiac.

Finally, the table shows the opposite of each star sign – this is the opposite sign in the astrological circle.

| Placed | Sign | Symbol | Element | Planet | Metal | Stone | Opposite |
|--------|------|--------|---------|--------|-------|-------|----------|
| 1 | Aries | Ram | Fire | Mars | Iron | Bloodstone | Libra |
| 2 | Taurus | Bull | Earth | Venus | Copper | Sapphire | Scorpio |
| 3 | Gemini | Twins | Air | Mercury | Mercury | Tiger's Eye | Sagittarius |
| 4 | Cancer | Crab | Water | Moon | Silver | Pearl | Capricorn |
| 5 | Leo | Lion | Fire | Sun | Gold | Ruby | Aquarius |
| 6 | Virgo | Maiden | Earth | Mercury | Mercury | Sardonyx | Pisces |
| 7 | Libra | Scales | Air | Venus | Copper | Sapphire | Aries |
| 8 | Scorpio | Scorpion | Water | Pluto | Plutonium | Jasper | Taurus |
| 9 | Sagittarius | Archer | Fire | Jupiter | Tin | Topaz | Gemini |
| 10 | Capricorn | Goat | Earth | Saturn | Lead | Black Onyx | Cancer |
| 11 | Aquarius | Waterbearer | Air | Uranus | Uranium | Amethyst | Leo |
| 12 | Pisces | Fishes | Water | Neptune | Tin | Moonstone | Virgo |